Any Ordinary Day

ALSO BY LEIGH SALES

On Doubt

Detainee 002: The Case of David Hicks

Any Ordinary Day

Leigh Sales

HAMISH HAMILTON
an imprint of
PENGUIN BOOKS

HAMISH HAMILTON

UK | USA | Canada | Ireland | Australia India | New Zealand | South Africa | China

Penguin Books is part of the Penguin Random House group of companies whose addresses
can be found at global.penguinrandomhouse.com.

Penguin
Random House
Australia

First published by Penguin Random House Australia Pty Ltd, 2018

Text copyright © Leigh Sales 2018

Cover design by Laura Thomas © Penguin Random House Australia Pty Ltd.
Cover image drawn by Laura Thomas from a photograph supplied by Stocksy
Typeset in Adobe Cason Pro 12/18 by Midland Typesetters, Australia.
Printed and bound in Australia by Griffin Press, an accredited ISO AS/NZS 14001
Environmental Management Systems printer.

 A catalogue record for this
book is available from the
National Library of Australia

ISBN: 978 0 14378 996 3

penguin.com.au

In Memory of Joseph Raymond Dale Sales

1948–2018

The very best of dads

Contents

Introduction

Staring at the Sun

The day that turns a life upside down usually starts like any other. You open your eyes, swing your body out of bed, eat breakfast, get dressed and leave the house, your mind busy. As you close the front door behind you, rarely is there a tingle of unease that something is off. Later, when the story of what happened next comes to be told, it will start with the day's deceptive ordinariness, something that will now seem incredible. How could a blindside so momentous have struck on a day that began so unremarkably?

In late 2014, the news media was dominated by two such days, so unimaginable in their endings that they rattled even those of us far removed from the events. On the afternoon of

November 25, a sparkling spring day, a young cricketer, Phillip Hughes, was fatally struck by a ball during a game. And on December 15, at morning tea time in a Sydney café, a gunman took eighteen people hostage, two of them – Katrina Dawson and Tori Johnson – killed by the siege's end.

Phillip Hughes had padded up as he'd done since childhood. Katrina Dawson had left her law office and popped downstairs for a hot chocolate. Tori Johnson had gone about his business on a regular day at work. Where was the last sign to exit the freeway, the chance to change course? It feels as if the universe cheated them by not warning that this was a day to stay home. If the universe – or fate, luck, God, happenstance, whatever you want to call it – didn't give them that courtesy, then it probably won't offer it to you or me either.

There are choices we all make in the full knowledge that they will alter the course of our lives: whether to marry or have children or change jobs. We expect such decisions to have consequences. The confronting thing about the cricket accident and the Lindt siege is that the choices leading to disaster were so minor they would have been barely worth contemplation. What family could imagine that sending their boy to cricket instead of soccer is a decision about how long he will live? Who could possibly function wondering each day if a decision about sharing a hot drink with a friend was a matter of life or death? We all make similar choices without pause every moment of every day, blessedly oblivious to where they might lead.

There's no way to stop the clandestine forces, marshalled by insignificant decisions, that will clash in a future instant. Some will have been on their trajectories for years, others for minutes. They level the rich and the poor, the weak and the powerful, without discrimination. It's straightforward to grasp this intellectually, but deeply emotionally uncomfortable to be prodded with the sharpness of the reality. The events in the news in late 2014 magnified the deepest truth of being alive, a fact that is both wonderful and terrible all at once – we never know what is coming next.

I have been a journalist for twenty-five years, and watching these kinds of indiscriminate tragedies play out is part of my professional life every day. From the very first newswriting lecture I attended, in February 1991 at the Queensland University of Technology, I knew I had found the right career for me. I loved everything about journalism: talking to people, writing stories, crafting headlines, editing text, and studying all sorts of different subjects under the pressure of a deadline. I would sit in the cafeteria at lunchtime with friends who were enrolled in law and accounting and think to myself with smug glee how dull their courses sounded by comparison. I still feel that way about journalism and I try not to take for granted how fortunate I am to have a job I enjoy so much.

As a young reporter, I was sent on every sort of story imaginable: floods, droughts, court cases, protest marches, police raids, murder trials, environmental messes, lunches for the homeless, colour features about the Royal Brisbane Show, surf accidents, sporting scandals, political downfalls. One thing

I quickly learned was that I was not one of those journalists who thrive chasing ambulances or disasters. I did not like coming face to face with tragedy or pain. I remember doing an overnight shift on the chief-of-staff desk at Channel Nine in 1994, and listening to the police scanner when two firefighters died battling a blaze in a Gold Coast home. The cameraman on the scene transmitted his footage back to me in the newsroom. He had captured their bodies being recovered from the house. My job was to make a list of all the key shots for the reporter who'd be assigned the story first thing in the morning: I was pretty certain that this was as close to death as I wanted to get. Over time, I gravitated to politics as much as possible, feeling more at ease dealing with a political tragedy than a genuine one.

I spent the first ten or so years of my career covering various news rounds and, amazingly, mostly managed to avoid firsthand exposure to true horror. I've never had to attend a car crash before the victims were cut from the vehicle, almost a rite of passage for many young journalists and police officers. I've never been sent to a war zone. I admire enormously my colleagues who do that sort of reporting because I know I do not have the courage or temperament for it.

From late 2001, just after the 9/11 terrorist attacks, I was the North America correspondent for the Australian Broadcasting Corporation. I didn't avoid disaster entirely (I was despatched to New Orleans to cover the calamitous Hurricane Katrina), but my stint there was heavily dominated by the politics of the wars in Iraq and Afghanistan and the imprisonment of an Australian, David Hicks, at the US military detention centre at Guantanamo Bay. I interviewed people who had lost family members in those wars and I visited Guantanamo a few times. For me it was not traumatic, because unlike the people I met and observed, I was able to return to my normal life after a few days.

For the past decade I've been largely studio-bound as an anchor, mostly on 7.30, the ABC's flagship nightly current affairs program. It is journalism of which I'm very proud and I could not have more respect for my colleagues. In my role, I sometimes interview people on the best days of their lives and often on the worst. I do so from the comfort and safety of an air-conditioned studio but it can still be painful, night after night, to immerse myself in the misery of the news. At least a couple of nights a week we run an item that comes close to reducing me to tears.

In one fairly typical news month on 7.30 – March 2016 – we covered child sex abuse by Catholic priests; coal workers dying horrible deaths from black lung; Fijian people devastated by a cyclone; nursing home residents abused by their carers; insurance companies refusing to pay people in dire need, even though they'd faithfully paid their premiums; a dance teacher who sexually abused children; a famous swimmer diagnosed with melanoma; five hundred people suddenly losing their jobs at an oil refinery; a suicide bombing in Turkey; students abducted by a Thai junta; a woman whose face was smashed with a hammer by her partner; a terrorist attack at Brussels airport; and a television star's degeneration from multiple sclerosis. Of course, there were other, happier stories too but the sad ones seem to make a stronger impact.

Notably, on the day of a terrorist attack, a mass-fatality accident or some other major news story, the number of viewers watching *7.30* will almost certainly be bigger than usual. A public disaster appears to make television ratings spike. People seem perversely but irresistibly attracted to catastrophe when it happens to others, while in our daily lives we do everything possible to shield ourselves from these poison darts of fate. We eat leafy green vegetables, apply sunscreen, wear seatbelts, obey speed limits, quit smoking, walk for half an hour a day, install spongy ground under monkey bars and swings, ban peanut butter sandwiches in schools, limit coffee intake, cut down on saturated fats, don bicycle helmets, submit to wanding, patting, screening and X-raying every time we fly, put non-slip mats in the shower, restrict ourselves to only one glass of red wine each day, and permit doctors to regularly scrape, probe and squeeze our private parts. It's as if we hope that watching others' misfortune might somehow teach us what new precautions we can add to our list to avoid the same fate.

I know rationally that the news is not a mirror held up to life. It is highly selective. (As one of my journalism lecturers told my class, ninety-nine helicopters might fly safely on any given day: what makes news is the one that did not.) Even so, reporting awful events for hours every day has made me fearful. In December 2014, I often lay awake at the thought of all the people who had recently found themselves in the news when their lives had been upended. I could scarcely bear to contemplate the questions those tragedies raised. Why them? Why not me? Why not somebody I love? When will it be my turn?

I felt an unshakable sense of dread that the wheel of fate had to be spinning for me too, the ball skipping towards my number.

Something had happened in my own life at the start of 2014 that changed me profoundly and undoubtedly contributed to my fear that my luck was running out. In February of that year, eight months pregnant, I woke one night with a sharp pain in my side and the sense that something was wrong. I already had one child, so I knew this wasn't labour pain.

I headed to the Royal Prince Alfred Hospital in Sydney and doctors ran various tests. The baby's heartbeat was fine and so were my vital signs but I was admitted for monitoring. There was some speculation about appendicitis. After a while, two ultrasound technicians arrived, and I could tell by their ashen faces as they looked at their screen that something was indeed wrong.

'What can you see?' I asked. At that stage, my pain was about three on a scale of ten.

'We can't see your organs,' one of the technicians replied. 'A dark substance is blocking the view.'

Even with my scant medical knowledge, I assumed that had to be blood.

My obstetrician arrived soon after and said something like: We don't know what's going on but I think we need to take you to the theatre for surgery, get the baby out, and once we can see what's happening, we'll call in whatever specialists are needed. He apologised, saying that instead of the usual small caesarean incision near the pubic bone, he would need to cut vertically up my abdomen so that he could have unimpeded access to all my abdominal organs. This would leave a large scar.

He left to scrub up and within a couple of minutes I was floored by utterly blinding pain. It went from a three to ten instantly and felt as if my ribs were cracking, one after the other. I tried not to breathe, as the slightest movement was excruciating. I still had the fetal heart rate monitor around my stomach and I heard the midwife say, 'I've lost the baby's heartbeat,' and she smacked a button on the wall.

I desperately wished to lose consciousness, partly to escape the physical pain but also because I was absolutely terrified. I had no idea what was going on. After the midwife triggered the alert, it seemed like pandemonium to me, although I assume that to a medical person it was not. I remember only snatches from then on: the agony as orderlies lifted me onto a gurney; the kindness of somebody reaching under the sheet and squeezing my hand as they ran down the corridor; the lights in the ceiling flashing rhythmically over my closed eyes as we raced under them; how I begged the anaesthetist to knock me out, not caring in all honesty if I died. She said something to the effect that it was less than ten seconds now, to just hold on.

The last thing I recall is seeing my obstetrician walk through the door in his scrubs as another person drew a line up my stomach with a marker where they were about to cut. Everything was moving so quickly, I feared they might start slicing before I was unconscious.

When I woke, there was no baby to be seen. I was on my back in a dimly lit room in what I learned was a high dependency unit.

I could sense that there was a tube going up one nostril. It was very uncomfortable and I was later told that it was running down the back of my throat into my stomach, pumping fluid out of it. Another tube snaked out of the bandages on my stomach, leeching brown fluid into a bag, and yet another tube fed into a catheter bag. I had oxygen prongs in my nostrils. Both hands had cannulas in them with even more tubes attached to drips on either side of the bed. My legs were in extremely tight white stockings. My left hand was wrapped around a plastic device with a button on it, and I quickly discovered that I would be knocked out if I pushed it enough times in a row.

I fell asleep again and the next time I woke, my obstetrician was there.

'Where's my baby?' I asked.

'He's in the neonatal intensive care unit,' the doctor replied, 'because he was deprived of oxygen for a period.' He told me that I'd had a uterine rupture.

I was reluctant to google those words for a long time after the event, but when I did, I read: 'Uterine rupture in pregnancy is a rare and often catastrophic complication with a high incidence of fetal and maternal morbidity . . . [T]he short time for instituting therapeutic action makes uterine rupture in pregnancy a much-feared event for medical practitioners.'

My obstetrician told me that when he opened my abdomen, it was a sea of blood. There was a tear the size of a cricket ball in the upper left side of my uterus. Due to the baby's traumatic birth, he didn't know if there had been brain damage or not, and wouldn't be able to tell for a while.

Whenever a baby is born, the nurses give it an Apgar score out of ten, measuring its vital signs. The test is done immediately after birth and then again five minutes later. My first child, born two years earlier in a natural delivery, was a 9 at birth and a 10 on the second check. This baby was a 2 at birth and then a 3 at five minutes.

I had lost a massive amount of blood, requiring three transfusions during surgery, and I was also numb with shock that the baby was in the neonatal intensive care unit with possible brain damage. When I broke down crying hysterically two days after surgery, the nurses took pity and wheeled me in my bed, trailing drips, bags and tubes, down to the NICU, where my baby was hooked up to all his paraphernalia. The first photograph of us together is the most pitiful sight imaginable. My son can barely be seen under the medical gear and I am unrecognisable. There was so much equipment attached to us both that instead of holding him, I just lay on the bed beside him.

That night, I had a terrible dream. I was in labour, frantically walking through a mansion, looking for a room in which to give birth. They were all locked or occupied and nobody would help. Another woman – a 'yummy mummy' with platinum-blond hair and a tidy bump out front – was also in labour, but handling it with ease. I kept trying to ask people, including her, for assistance but I couldn't speak properly and nobody could understand what I was saying.

The sound of my own voice in the hospital room woke me up. I was crying out, 'Mummy, Mummy, Mummy!' and tears were streaming down my cheeks.

That was possibly the single most devastating moment out of everything that had happened, worse than the pain and fear I'd experienced. I had been reduced to this pathetic, childlike state, begging for my own mother to come and save me. I have never even called my mother 'Mummy'! She had rung me that very day to ask if she should come down from Queensland and I was adamant that she should not, because I didn't want to be a bother.

Somehow, although my intellect didn't understand it, my subconscious knew that I had entirely lost my sense of security in the world, and, to a degree, my sense of self. Here was I, this supposedly competent, independent person, not only unable to look after myself, but unable to care for my own children. My dream shattered me because it made me feel that the person I considered myself to be – self-sufficient, in control – was not, in fact, who I had turned out to be. Although I knew it was irrational, I felt ashamed and weak. It was terrifying.

Even as I grew well again over the months that followed, and it became clear that my baby was fine, the whole experience felt like I had tumbled into a raging river. I feared I would not make it to the other side. I tried to swim back to where I'd started but the current was too strong. Sometimes I lost my grip and the torrent swept me along. Finally, I clambered onto the opposite bank and collapsed. I could see the place I had started from but I could not get back there. The view of my life where I had come ashore was not the same as the view from where I had set off. The world did not seem as safe as it once had, and the possibility of death or catastrophe seemed real, not distant things I didn't need to worry about for the time being.

The experience amplified for me the questions with which the news confronts me every night: How do we come to terms with the fact that life can blindside us in an instant? When the unthinkable does happen, what comes next? How does a person go on? Do we, as a community, have a responsibility to people who unwittingly find themselves in the middle of a story that we all want to know more about? And once we truly understand that we are not exceptional, but are instead as vulnerable as the next person, what does that tell us about how we should live?

All of us will experience grief and suffering. It is part of the human package. I dread the anticipated losses of life – the deaths of my parents, the slow decline of age – but those prospects don't terrify me as much as something unexpected that turns life upside down instantly. I have spent much of my career trying to avoid direct exposure to those events. My own life in 2014, plus the news stories I anchored afterwards, made me realise that avoidance is pointless. It is trying to hide from life itself.

What prompted me to begin writing this book was the thought of what might happen if I walked towards what I most feared, rather than in the opposite direction. What would I learn if I spent time with people who had lived through some of the things I most worried about happening to me or my family? What could the newest scientific research teach me about the way the human brain comes to terms with such things? The novelist Iris Murdoch once wrote that paying attention is a moral act. To me, paying close attention to these kinds of tragedies felt like staring at the sun. It scared me to do it, yet I wanted to see what would happen if I didn't look away.

One

That Could Have Been Me

I'm sure I'm not the only person to watch something awful on the news and think, *That could have been me*. But what is the actual chance that you or I could be swept up in a tragic event of the kind that makes headlines and permanently transforms our lives?

One morning while I mull this question, I stop by the Lindt Café in Sydney for a cappuccino. Instead of powder, coarse flakes of Swiss chocolate float on top of the coffee. It's delicious, and I drink it sitting at a table with my back to enormous windows that front the outdoor plaza of Martin Place. Along another wall are glass cabinets with thousands of brightly wrapped chocolate balls and gift boxes tied with ribbon. Rainbow-hued macarons line up in a display case under the cash register, and the ding of a counter bell punctuates the hiss of the coffee machine every time an order is ready.

The café patrons are as varied as the goodies on sale – young, old, frail, professional, touristy, weather-beaten, solitary, convivial. At one table, a thirtyish businessman methodically polishes his glasses with a handkerchief, an act so old-fashioned in a young person that it both charms and jars.

A few blocks from the colourful Lindt Café is a courtroom whose colours run the full spectrum from light brown to dark brown. On the same morning that I sit sipping my coffee, eighteen people, just as diverse as those sitting around me, are having a very different experience. One by one, they are stepping into the witness box at a coronial inquest. Nearly two years earlier, on a very similar day, they too had been at the Lindt Café; sadly, they experienced one of those days that begin ordinarily enough but don't end that way. Some of them were staff at the café, others were meeting friends or on a break from work.

These strangers were forever united when a gunman, claiming to have explosives in his backpack, took them hostage. Man Haron Monis had a long history of violence and an affinity with the murderous Islamic State movement. He terrorised the group in the café for sixteen hours, all of it broadcast live on television by cameras trained on the building. During the siege, many of the hostages escaped through various exits, but at 2.14 am, with five hostages still trapped, Monis executed one of them, the café's manager, Tori Johnson. Hearing the gunshot, police burst through the doors in a hail of bullets and glass. A café patron, Katrina Dawson, was killed. The three remaining hostages survived their injuries, but everyone in the café that day, even the people who escaped early, was left with lasting trauma.

I drink my coffee in the exact place where that all happened and I dwell on it. Why is it that the people I'm with get to enjoy morning tea and then go about their business, but the others did not? A café is so non-threatening and familiar a setting that the Lindt siege caused most Australians to feel rattled and unsafe, even if they were nowhere near the place at the time. This is a common reaction to major disasters, and the more regular the scene of a catastrophe, the more our collective sense of security is undermined. The tragedy feels too close for comfort.

But when we look at the facts, not just our feelings, what are the genuine odds of an awful, random event ensnaring us individually? And are the things we most fear happening to us the things of which we should be most afraid?

In September 2002, Louisa Hope was diagnosed with multiple sclerosis. As if that wasn't enough bad news for a lifetime, in December 2014 she was a Lindt Café hostage. The chance of any Australian having the remarkable misfortune to tick both those boxes is one in 1.39 billion.

'Oh, I'm so glad you worked that out,' Louisa exclaims as we share a beetroot salad for lunch at my house. 'I've been saying I wish I knew an actuary who could run the stats for me.'

Louisa is a vivacious 54-year-old, a large woman with wavy chestnut hair and a face like a porcelain doll: creamy skin, brown eyes, rosebud lips. She had arrived laden with treats for me – chocolate-coated cherries, loose-leaf tea and a colourful mug – a gesture made sweeter by the fact that she was already being very generous by letting me pry into some of the most difficult moments of her life.

If anybody's entitled to feel victimised by misfortune, it's Louisa. Should I be diagnosed with MS, I would think that entitled me to a leave pass from further misfortune for the rest of my life, never mind finding myself part of a terrorist attack. I suspect my fury and indignation, were I in her position, would be boundless. I want Louisa to help me understand how somebody comes to terms with being singled out this way.

Louisa's MS diagnosis came about thanks to a sore back. She'd had a few falls, putting them down to bad luck and high heels. When she visited a chiropractor for some relief, he urged her to see a neurologist, fearing something more sinister than clumsiness. The specialist sent her for an MRI, and soon after delivered the terrible blow: Louisa's falls were caused by multiple sclerosis, an incurable disease of the central nervous system that affects the brain and spinal cord.

'Did you know anything about MS at the time?' I ask her.

'No. But when I was a child, there was a lady right next door, a young woman, and she was in a wheelchair. I have the most vivid memories of her life, she was very disabled. She used to send us up the road to buy her cigarettes and then we'd come back and we'd have to light the cigarette for her. It was so exciting, we loved that,' Louisa recalls. After her own diagnosis, her mother had told her, 'You know, Noelene had MS.'

Louisa says, 'I was like, "What?" I remembered she went away and had to be looked after in some special place for people with MS and she died. I was thinking, Wheelchair, right, that's it, that's my future.'

Today, fourteen years after her diagnosis, Louisa walks slowly with the aid of a cane. She may maintain her mobility for many years, or things could change suddenly for the worse. MS is an insidious disease because it's impossible to know how it will proceed in any one case. Sometimes it's aggressive, but sometimes the decline is very gradual and a sufferer can slide in and out of remission for years.

The same month that Louisa was diagnosed, she was whacked with two other blows: she turned forty and her husband divorced her.

'You don't imagine a future that's full of crap, but there you go!' she laughs.

'When this cluster of events happened all at once, did you think, Why me, it's not fair?' I ask. 'How did you process it?'

Louisa thinks for a few moments. 'It was shocking and life-changing, it really was. It's like you're standing on a shore watching the ocean suck the life right out of you. But the truth is, I believe in God, I have a personal faith, and I had to just rely on that. It was like, I have to trust God's best intention for my life. Otherwise I would have just fallen into a screaming heap.'

When Louisa says this, my heart sinks. I flirted with religion in my late teens and early twenties but ultimately, I just couldn't buy the dogma. It seemed irrational to me that people who didn't believe the same things that I did were going to hell. I saw too much hypocrisy in supposed Christians who said one thing and did another. And now I wonder if anyone can really be at ease with having MS and being a victim of a terrorist attack by believing it's God's will. I'm very sceptical. It can't be that simple.

No sooner do I have these thoughts than I'm irritated with myself. Who do I think I am, judging somebody in Louisa's position? It's presumptuous. I'm never going to learn anything useful if the first time somebody trusts me enough to let me into their thinking, I immediately close my mind to what they're offering. I hope my internal reaction hasn't showed on my face. I really do want to understand how Louisa has dealt with what's happened in her life, and the only way I can do that is by drilling down into what she believes.

'But didn't you think, Why, God, why are you doing this to me?' I hope I'm not offending her with my blunt questions.

'No, it never was Why, God? or Why me?' Louisa says emphatically. 'I remember once at work, before all this, I was working on reception and someone came in. They had a walking stick. They were much older than they should have been, I could tell that. They felt sorry for themselves, they were very filled with self-pity. You could just feel it. I wondered what had happened to that person that they had reached that stage, and I thought, That will never happen to me. But at the same time, I thought, What makes you imagine that won't happen to you? Why wouldn't bad things happen to you? It was like this moment where I thought,

Huh, that's right. So when I was diagnosed with MS, Why me? wasn't a question.'

'You already had an understanding that you're as vulnerable as the next person?' I ask.

'I really did,' she replies.

I am still very sceptical that Louisa's faith meant she could calmly accept having multiple sclerosis. As we talk, it becomes clear that I'm jumping to false conclusions based on my own dismissive view of religion. Of course Louisa wasn't calm, especially at the beginning. Her beliefs don't inoculate her every second of the day from fear and anger.

'It was scary. It was a dark time, this new reality I had to come to terms with. But the thing was, I really didn't want to go down some rabbit hole of self-pity and resentment and just general insanity. I wanted to avoid that so much, and so at first, I had this thing where I would only allow myself one hour every day to think about the MS and my divorce and all the other random things you dwell on when your life has just disintegrated. At first, I couldn't wait for that hour so I could just cry and rage and freak out in the privacy of my own head. But over time, as I prayed and meditated and the days rolled into months, I couldn't wait for the hour to be over, and then it got shorter and shorter and then I didn't do it anymore.'

'What about being alone – were you worried about who would look after you if the MS got bad?'

'No,' she says, 'that was always okay. I knew I'd be looked after. I have great friends and a good church community and my family is loving and caring, they would always be there for me.'

Louisa's 72-year-old mother, Robin, was with her on the morning of the Lindt siege. They were in the city for an appointment in the same building as the café. The women were running early, so they decided to stop for coffee. As Louisa went to the cash register to pay, she saw that some of the other customers were flustered that the café doors wouldn't open. The girl behind the counter seemed vague and distracted.

'I went back and sat down with my mum and I said, "The doors are stuck, I think I'd better go and speak to somebody about this door situation." I mean, we weren't in a desperate hurry, we figured it was just some little alarm thing. But then *he* stood up,' Louisa says.

It was Man Haron Monis. Louisa had noticed him earlier, when he had been sitting at a table near her and Robin. Now he was towards the front of the café.

'He stood up and he said, "Okay." I can't remember exactly what he said, but he may have said, "I'm taking you hostage." He had his gun and then he started to say in a very calm and soft voice that he had two bombs in his backpack and there were other bombs around the city. Then he started to direct people. And it's very real at that point, you know,' Louisa says.

The hostages were ordered to hold Islamic flags in the window and to ring high-profile media outlets. During the ensuing sixteen hours, Monis swung between acts of benevolence, such as allowing Louisa to take her medicine, and extreme hostility.

'Once the initial shock settled and the hours passed,' I say, 'did you think, Oh God, give me a break, I've got MS and now I have to be a hostage in a terrorist situation?'

'No, actually my thought was: Oh God, give me a break, my mother's here with me. I'm going to have to look after her. Not that I have any problems looking after her,' Louisa adds, 'but I just knew how hard it was going to be. It didn't take too long to work out that he [Monis] was that classic dude, the one that bashes his wife and then says, "I love you," at the same time. He needed the women to be submissive. Robin was quite back-chatty and that was quite distressing.'

The mood among the hostages, perhaps surprisingly, mostly remained very calm for the duration of the siege. Nobody wanted to do anything to upset Monis or make things worse. That's not to say the situation wasn't utterly terrifying. In the early hours of the morning, a group of hostages escaped. Louisa was not far from the door herself, and for a split second thought she could make it out too. With difficulty, she started walking towards the exit, but then she thought of her mother and stopped. Louisa knew she couldn't live with herself if she left Robin behind. As she stopped walking, she expected Monis to shoot her in the back and so she crumpled to the floor, face down, believing her death was imminent.

'My mind is saying, Okay, look at this situation – oh no, you're not getting out of this one. For me, I always understood intellectually that we have a spirit and we have a mind and we have emotions. But in the siege, I understood this for the first time within myself, in my gut. There was this voice telling me not to be afraid. There's no fear, it's peace, absolute peace,' she says. 'There was a battle within my mind, yes – I would have liked to not get killed by this mongrel. But emotionally, I've gone through the battle of surrendering to my spirit' – Louisa means because of her religious belief and adapting to MS – 'and yes, I'm okay that I die. If that's the way it's got to be, that's it.'

The next thing, Monis was dragging her to her feet. She will never know why he chose to let her live. Not long after, he executed Tori Johnson, triggering the police bombardment. When the police burst in, Monis had positioned Louisa and Robin on either side of him, perhaps intending them to be shields. With deafening gunfire exploding around her, Louisa fell down again, certain for the second time that she was about to die.

'They're coming in the door. Me, Man Monis, [there's] like a foot between us. When you're in there, the bullets . . . it's all going insane. Monis is dead. Katrina is dead. How am I not dead? That's a serious question,' Louisa says.

'Because of your faith, do you believe there's a reason for that? Do you believe that God chose to let you live?'

'I don't have that sense. There is an absolute ratbag delusion of "God chose me" and there's a dangerous element to the concept that "I'm special to God". So many people have said to me, "You were saved for a reason," and all that kind of stuff. Maybe.' Louisa sounds as if this might be something she's still puzzling through herself.

During the gunfight that ended the siege, Louisa was pelted by shrapnel, including a particularly nasty piece that embedded in her left foot. An ambulance rushed her to hospital, where she endured three operations during a three-month stay. After we finish our lunch, Louisa removes her sandal and pulls down a pressure bandage, showing me a giant, scarred hole, basically covering the entire arch of her foot.

'This foot is what they call the MS drop foot,' she tells me. 'This was my dodgy foot anyway. How fortunate am I that if I was going to get an injury, it's in my dodgy foot?'

'This was just from shrapnel?' I'm shocked at the size of the scar.

'Just from shrapnel. I got shrapnel in my body too. I've got two scars, one that looks like it was done by French nuns and one that looks like it was done by German butchers. One of the pieces of shrapnel, they couldn't get it out. The doctor came around and she was like, "I'm so sorry," and she was so intensely conveying her disappointment that I just randomly said to her, "Oh doc, what a shame you couldn't have done a bit of lipo[suction] while you were down there!" And she chastised me and said, "Louisa, your fat saved your life." I think sometimes, things that you think you don't like about yourself or someone else, you don't know how this sets you up for future salvation in some way. You know, the MS in itself, having MS and all the physical trauma involved in that, prepared me for the three months in hospital. I knew how to sit and get better and wait for things to fix and not go crazy.'

'Do you ever wish God could give you just a bit less of the . . .' I pause, because the word I'm thinking of is 'suffering'. Although it's obvious Louisa has suffered enormously, I feel awkward about saying that out loud to her.

Louisa doesn't share my discomfort at confronting this question head-on.

'Yeah, I'm often like, God, could I just learn the lesson quickly? But when the random bad stuff happens, it's like, Okay, what's the lesson? What good am I going to be able to suck out of this that's going to grow me?'

Louisa's positive attitude, born of her conviction that God has a plan for her, is admirable but I still have a hard time thinking the way she does.

'If having MS prepared you for being injured in a hostage situation, I'm really scared to imagine what the Lindt siege is preparing you for,' I put to her. 'How do you wrap your head around the randomness of things? I know you believe in God but the future is so unknown.'

'This is the thing. We live in a myth that it's not. We live imagining that there are certainties. That's just this big, collective lie that we live in. We're so caught up in the state of our Western culture – we can make this happen, we can affect that, we can do this, we can do that. We can create our safe world. Then along comes some nasty terrorist and blows it up. It's a collective delusion.' Louisa pauses. 'I don't say this too loudly because most people can't handle me saying it, but it's like a gift to be reminded that life can change, that we're not in control. To have that shockingly ripped from you, it is a gift. You go, Right, okay.'

'I'd better live more fully?' I suggest.

'That's right and it's very humbling. It's not my plan, but tomorrow if you hear news that I've died in some bizarre and mysterious way, it's okay,' she tells me.

It strikes me that Louisa has a very unique combination of beliefs. She lives her life trusting that God is in control of it but she also has an acute understanding that everything is fragile and uncertain, as if God doesn't exist and things are utterly random. There's no doubt that whatever it is she believes, it's given her extraordinary resilience as she's flipped over one bad hand of cards after another.

I'm very glad to say that in the months since Louisa and I had lunch, she has not died in some bizarre and mysterious way. She's busy and content and we exchange friendly emails from time to time. Our conversation caused me to think deeply about the ways people cope with life's blows, especially her insight that it's a fantasy to imagine we have any control or any magical protection from bad things happening to us. Louisa's logic is irrefutable and I know what she says is true. That doesn't stop it from scaring me, or mean I'm keen to accept it.

As a journalist, I rely on a particular skill set when I want to find something out. I'm good at tracking people down. I know how to craft a line of questioning that helps them open up. I'm a strong listener and I follow up what people are saying. I can connect dots and identify interesting anecdotes. Those are handy tools, but even before meeting Louisa I'd already suspected that to find answers about the probability of being caught up in a newsworthy blindside, and how people react, I'd need more in my kit than that. I'd have to undertake real research, of the kind an expert would do, and that was out of my comfort zone.

I'm not an academic or a specialist in any field, so I wasn't quite sure where to even start looking. I rang my friend Cathy, who's a research librarian and an expert at navigating databases and book collections around the world. Her business card should say *I Find Stuff That You Can't.*

'If I pay you to work on your day off for a few months, do you reckon you can help me?' I asked her.

She agreed and I gave her the broadest, most nebulous brief imaginable. I was slightly embarrassed by how imprecise it was but she seemed up for the challenge. She came around to my house one morning and installed some software called Mendeley on my laptop. This is a system for organising academic papers, and before I knew it she had indexed hundreds of journal articles under tags, such as 'trauma', 'grief', 'adaptation', 'blame', 'memory', and 'survival'.

The reading Cathy prescribed for me proved hard work. There was plenty of maths, especially probability and statistics. I started by plucking out articles that seemed to look at the big picture: history and psychology and the science of how our brains work. Something started to take shape; it was clear that discomfort about what the future might hold, and finding ways to eliminate that uncertainty, cuts across almost every academic discipline, from maths to biology to economics.

For all recorded time, human beings have been fascinated by the intersection of destiny and chance and have craved ways to test and tame the Fates. We hate to feel vulnerable, and seek reassurance any way we can. We read horoscopes, pray to gods, visit clairvoyants, consult tarot cards, check weather forecasts, and scour news stories about our risk of contracting various diseases so we can take the necessary precautions against them.

Gambling can be dated back to 3500 BC, thanks to an ancient form of dice uncovered during an archaeological dig in Egypt. And gamblers, along with people whose jobs involve precision, luck or high risk, such as sports stars, actors, soldiers and sailors, frequently turn to superstitious rituals for protection. It's not just them either. I can't tell you how many times I've approached a red traffic light and thought something like, If it turns green before I stop the car, I'll pass the exam. And if I end up stopping the car? Okay, best of three.

Every day we ascribe significance to the most random, meaningless events so as to give ourselves a sense of control over our world. Human brains have evolved to need predictability. Our ancient ancestors had to make dozens of decisions every day that went to their very survival – what food was good to eat, what shelter would offer the best protection from the elements, what locations were safe from predators. Predictability was useful because it streamlined the decision-making process: if a plant had been safely eaten previously, it could be safely eaten again. The need for predictability was so strong that evolutionary biology caused our brains to permanently prefer it.

The brain gathers all sorts of data from the outside world and stores it as memories. Memories then help us to make decisions about how to act, by evaluating past experience against present reality. That mental process occurs in a split second for something as simple as climbing a set of stairs, but it can be more tortuous for complicated decisions, such as whether another person is trustworthy. The brain particularly loves patterns it can recognise because they foster predictability in the world around us and help eliminate unpleasant feelings of insecurity or unfamiliarity.

Many scientific experiments have demonstrated the brain's preference for predictability over unpredictability. In one study, monkeys were given the option of two coloured targets, both of which came with rewards but only one of which gave advance information about what that reward would be. After a few days, the monkeys showed a clear preference for the target that gave information about the future. In another experiment, humans were found to prefer receiving a guaranteed electric shock over sitting with the uncertainty that they might or might not get a shock. In other words, people feel better about knowing what is coming – even if it is painful – than not knowing. It's easier to prepare ourselves when we know what's in store, whether it's good or bad. There is thus a biological basis to the cliché 'forewarned is forearmed'.

There is also a chemical reason for this preference for certainty and predictability. When our brains receive information that 'makes sense', they behave in the same way as when we satisfy any other craving: by releasing dopamine, a chemical that makes us feel pleasure. With dopamine, the body feels calm, content, comfortable, relieved and safe. By contrast, uncertainty feels closer to pain and the body tries to avoid it. People have varying levels of tolerance for the feeling of uncertainty. Somebody with obsessive-compulsive disorder, for example, has an extreme aversion to it.

The human bias towards predictability causes us to look for cause and effect in the world around us, even for things that defy easy explanation. The idea that everything happens for a reason is a reassuring thought, as if somewhere out there is a blueprint, dictating the course of our lives, even if we can't see it. A sense of certainty comes with believing that things are under some form of control, whether somebody else's or our own. For many people it's comforting to believe that factors such as how hard we work, the choices we make, or the goodness of our deeds influence our destiny more than luck and chance do.

Does this kind of thinking square with the evidence, though? Many life-changing events – and even everyday ones – are arbitrary. Did Louisa do something that meant she 'deserved' MS? Of course not. Neither did she deserve to have the misfortune to be one of the eighteen people in the Lindt Café while you or I were not. Why was it that Louisa lived but Tori and Katrina died? The brain wants an explanation so it can satisfy its desire for cause and effect. Something like the Lindt siege shatters our individual feeling of security and the brain desperately wants that restored. Such events don't come with a ready explanation and yet the brain still hunts for one. It needs an answer so it can file the experience away and move on to thinking about less threatening things, like what to cook for dinner.

When the brain grapples with why something happened, or thinks, That could have been me, it relies on its usual device of searching for familiar patterns so it can help settle on an explanation with which to feel comfortable. My reading has led me to believe that in this quest, the brain is largely influenced by three things: past personal experience, evolutionary biology, and the experiences of others, this last often conveyed to us via the news media. Superficially, each of these things feels like it should be a sound guide. Actually, our bias towards predictability and explanation means that often we see what we want to believe rather than reality.

Personal experience – being what we've directly seen and felt – is hard to accept as unreliable. Yet our brains' habits can trick us. Our desire for cause and effect inclines us to see connections where there are none. Take coincidence. You can find whole books devoted to extraordinary real-life coincidences, because they suggest there is more to life than random chance and serendipity. We love those stories. My car breaks down and I take the bus and I sit next to a stranger who becomes my future husband. The car was 'meant' to malfunction. It was destiny. Forget all the other times I've taken the bus uneventfully. The brain is disinclined to remember the dozens of unremarkable occurrences because it's hardwired to remember the single unusual one (because it deviates from the predictable and therefore could be a threat to survival).

The more extraordinary the coincidence, the more unpredictable the event, and the greater the significance that the brain attributes to it. After the Lindt siege, there were numerous anecdotes from people who reported that they had left the café only minutes earlier, or they'd meant to go there that very morning but had a last-minute change of plans. Humans crave these tales of near misses, of signs heeded or fate cheated, because they assure us that our lives are special, that our existence has a unique significance to the universe, just as it has to ourselves. Such stories almost always appear after a disaster, including the sinking of the *Titanic* in 1912, after which Michigan's *Sault Ste Marie Evening News* reported on the 7000-odd members of the 'just missed it' club, noting that most had 'engaged passage but cancelled their reservations' and that several hundred had 'premonitions of disaster'.

There is a certain narcissism in this kind of thinking – or, as Louisa Hope puts it, 'an absolute ratbag delusion'. It is patently ludicrous that the person who skipped their morning coffee on the day of the Lindt Café siege was special enough to be spared but Louisa and the other seventeen hostages were not.

Most unusual events, like being the victim of a terrorist attack, can be at least partially explained thanks to a mathematical theory called the Law of Large Numbers. When you take an enormous group of people (a 'sample'), the chance of an extremely rare event occurring is greatly magnified. A one-in-a-million chance of something happening might seem very unlikely. Yet Australia's population is 24 million: if every year, just a single one-in-a-million event happens somewhere in the country, twenty-four Australians will be that one.

The Law of Large Numbers explains why something that might feel highly significant to you personally may not in fact be unique. Say you dream that a friend died and the next day you find out that the friend has indeed passed away. No doubt you would find that coincidence highly memorable and think it meant something. Yet in 2003 a British statistician calculated the odds of dreaming about a friend's death on the night it actually happens. He based his maths on Britain's population at the time, 55 million (a gigantic sample), and assumed an average of one dream of a friend's death per lifetime. He then factored in the national death rate of 2000 every 24 hours. Crunching those numbers, the odds of an accurate death dream in Britain are one every two weeks.

Given the size of the global population (7.5 billion), the Law of Large Numbers means that Lindt Café-type events are sadly common. What it doesn't mean is that we are more likely to be caught in one ourselves. Our planet is the ultimate large sample. With so many of us, one individual's chance of being the victim of the kind of blindside that lands in the news is still small. Our brains make the prospect seem more likely than it really is because they're putting unusual events – the ones that defy past patterns – in neon lights.

If the chance of awful, random disasters affecting us personally is remote, why are we so rattled by them? And why do we worry so much about them happening to us? As with the brain's preference for predictability, the answer lies in evolutionary biology, which, along with our personal experience, is often a key reason we draw the conclusions we do. Until about a millisecond ago, in terms of the span of human history, we lived together in small tribes. We stayed with the same people from birth to death. Our ancestors faced potentially catastrophic threats from things that are no longer much of a problem for most of us in the modern world: snakes, spiders, large cats and other predators, darkness, being alone, being exposed in an open place. Over many centuries, humans evolved to internalise the fear of those things, and today they remain some of our most common fears.

Our ancestors had great cause to fear situations that could claim many lives at once, and possibly wipe out most of a tribe's population. Safety was in numbers, and the chances of survival improved with the size of the tribe. New threats, or those that had never been previously experienced, were also particularly terrifying, because the tribe could not prepare a response. Humans living today are genetically programmed through evolution to fear blindsides and disasters that result in mass casualties.

By looking at how our brains have evolved, scientists and psychologists have been able to map many of our common fears according to what they call 'dread risk'. An event that is uncontrollable, unfair, unfamiliar, unimaginable, that causes huge suffering or leads to multiple fatalities and widespread destruction, is considered to have high dread risk. Events with high dread risk include chemical warfare, terrorism and gun massacres. Low dread risk events include smoking and falls from ladders. Thanks to biology, events with a high dread risk scare us more than those with a low one, even though the low are statistically more likely to cause death or injury. We know the dangers of smoking and climbing ladders but these feel like things we can control, unlike the question of when or where a terrorist might detonate a bomb.

The high dread risk of situations that claim many lives at once versus the low dread risk of things that cause more deaths spread over time is why many of us are more scared of the plane flight than the drive to the airport, despite the latter being statistically a far greater danger. It's what makes nuclear accidents more gut-churning than obesity. We watch an event like the Lindt Café siege on the news and feel extremely vulnerable, even though the more probable risk to our personal longevity is the bowl of chips and the bottle of wine we consume while sitting in front of the TV. Our reaction is due to the ancient threats our ancestors faced and the way we're wired as a result.

The news media reinforces both dread risk and the brain's propensity to emphasise unusual events. The media is like the human brain writ large, relegating ordinary, everyday occurrences in favour of rare ones. If you often watch the news, you may come to believe that the events that are reported (terrorist attacks, shark maulings, child abductions) are more common than they really are. You might even come to think that such things are credible threats in your own life, thanks to the way you're evolutionally designed to be on particular alert for mass casualty events and blindsides. You are instinctively protective of your 'tribe' and not intuitively likely to put the awful event into the context of the Law of Large Numbers.

Technology has also made the world more interconnected than ever and so the sample size for horrible events is simply gigantic. TV news is especially powerful because the image of one murdered child and his sobbing parents will make a far greater impact on you than the knowledge that millions of children played safely on the same day. The news doesn't help you assess the gravest risks to your safety; instead, it distracts you from them by redirecting your fears to things that do not place you in much personal danger at all.

The way that our individual experiences, evolutionary biology and the news media mislead us means that most of the time when we think, That could have been me, we are most probably wrong. Even worse, those false conclusions can sometimes pose hazards almost as serious as the threat itself. In the months after the September 2001 terrorist attacks in the United States, Americans were afraid to fly and so planes carried about 17 per cent fewer passengers compared with the same period before the attacks. Instead, the number of miles driven increased by about 5 per cent, according to US government estimates. A 2006 study by three professors at Cornell University calculated that in the two years after 9/11, an estimated 2302 additional people were likely killed because they drove instead of flew (only 700 or so fewer than died in the terrorist attacks).

I fell into this kind of thinking myself in the midst of researching this chapter, when you might imagine I would have been more attuned to the pitfalls of irrational thinking. News came through of a terrible tragedy at the Dreamworld theme park on the Gold Coast. Four people were killed in a gruesome accident when one of the most popular rides malfunctioned. Like the Lindt Café siege, the event sent the community into deep shock. Many Australians have visited Dreamworld and so they felt vulnerable. I was as disturbed as anyone and that afternoon, when I picked up my children from their day care centre, I thought, I don't want the boys to ever go on amusement park rides. I reached this dubious snap conclusion as I drove them home in my car.

Yet in 2016, only four Australians died on amusement park rides (the group at Dreamworld) while more than a thousand died in car accidents. My sons would be vastly safer on a rollercoaster than letting me drive them around. Still, the way I figured it, rollercoasters were a risk I could avoid. Getting rid of my car would be extremely inconvenient, so I was prepared to chance it.

My thought process about not letting my children go on rollercoasters is so common that there's a name for it: minimax regret. Mathematicians in a field called decision theory use the term to describe behaviour whereby you make a choice based on an evaluation of what you might regret later. I want to avoid rollercoasters in case I later regret injury to my children: that type of thinking applies minimax regret. Even the brain's seemingly quirkiest behaviour is more predictable than most of us probably realise.

It's not only individuals like me who think and act illogically in this regard, governments sometimes do it too. The top three causes of death in Australia each have low dread risk: heart disease, dementia and stroke. In 2014, the year of the Lindt Café siege, around one in a thousand Australians died from heart disease. By contrast, the odds of any single Australian being one of the hostages killed in the Lindt Café was roughly one in 12 million. Put another way, the risk of dying that year from a heart attack was twelve thousand times greater than being killed in the Lindt siege. Even though the risk to Australians from heart disease dramatically outweighs the risk from terrorism, how much does the government spend combating and treating cardiovascular disease? Around 7 billion dollars each year. How much does it spend on national security, law enforcement and counterterrorism efforts? More than five times that, at around 35 billion dollars.

We partly accept such an allocation of resources because of our dread risk: terrorism scares us more than heart disease. We also realise that the gap between deaths from heart disease and deaths from terrorism would probably shrink if we spent fewer dollars on counterterrorism.

Another reason relates to the same thinking that compels many of us to buy home insurance, even if the chance of our house burning to the ground or being destroyed in some other disaster is very slim. We cannot stomach the risk of being the one in the one-in-a-million probability ratio. We prefer to take a gamble that has 100 per cent odds on a small loss (the cost of the premium) over the unknown chance of a ruinous loss (of the entire house). Most insurance policies are taken out on the grounds of consequence, not probability – the same reason I'm now scared about my boys going on theme park rides. I know that it's highly improbable that something bad will happen and yet my fear of the consequences overrides my logic. My brain is trying to impose certainty and order by ruling out the possibility of my sons being killed in a freak accident.

Yet, as Louisa Hope points out, it's a delusion to think that we can avoid bad things happening to us. I can't possibly imagine and pre-empt every tragedy that might befall my sons. They may not die on a rollercoaster, but any number of other catastrophes could head their way, none of which I will see coming.

Experts call those type of blindsides black swans. An American writer, Nassim Taleb, coined the name to refer to a high-impact, rare, and hard-to-imagine event. The term references those British explorers who arrived in Australia and saw black swans for first time, having only ever seen white ones. Hurricane Katrina, which devastated New Orleans in 2005 and killed more than 1300 people in the most destructive natural disaster in American history, was a black swan. So was 9/11. Not every natural disaster or terrorist attack is a black swan. They have to reach a magnitude so huge that they're beyond the scale of what anyone has ever imagined or anticipated.

Nobody can predict specific black swans, but every competent business or government knows they are a general threat, and big organisations war-game generic, worst-case scenarios. The difficulty is that the more complex a system, the harder it is to make accurate forecasts and control uncertainty. There is nothing more complex than an individual life, with its large number of social links and countless tiny decisions that ripple through the years, determining its course. All that individuals, businesses and governments can do is hope for the best and try to guard against the worst.

It's both reassuring and unsettling to learn all of this. Using cold hard logic, I understand that the chance of a random disaster personally ensnaring me is remote. The events in the stories I present on television that most disturb me are the ones least likely to happen to me or my family. And yet that's not as comforting as it should be, for a simple reason: I've met Louisa Hope and she has made me acutely aware that somebody is always the one in the probability ratio, even when the odds are as remote as one in 1.39 billion.

From the reading list Cathy has given me, it quickly becomes obvious that life's blindsides and what they tell us about ourselves isn't something that fits neatly into any one field of study. There's wisdom to be gleaned from almost every discipline – psychology, neurology, mathematics, philosophy, literature, science, religion. Even the law constantly deals with questions of fairness and chance. The journalist in me craves the experience of being able to talk to people about these things. I yearn to speak with somebody whose job cuts across a lot of different areas of expertise, in the hope that there's a way to survey the entire landscape at once. I need a compass for my navigation.

Many years ago, I attended a dinner at which I sat next to the vice-chancellor of the University of Sydney, Michael Spence. I've remembered it for two reasons. One is that I very much enjoyed the company of Michael and his wife, Beth. The second is that I was saddened to read in the newspaper not long afterwards that she had died of cancer, leaving him widowed with five children.

It strikes me now that Michael Spence might be the right person to help me. Losing his wife will have undoubtedly given him personal insight into some of my questions, but his job running a university also means he must have a good grasp of a broad range of subjects. I google Michael and read that he has many academic specialties: English, Italian, law, and theology. He is also an ordained Anglican minister.

He agrees to meet, and so on a slightly chilly, overcast day, I walk through one of the most beautiful spaces in Australia, the University of Sydney's quadrangle. The green square is surrounded on all sides by ornate buildings that would make an ideal setting for Harry Potter. The vice-chancellor's office, tucked into the bottom corner of one of these buildings, is a giant, wood-panelled room with high ceilings. On one side, enormous windows look out into the quadrangle. The opposite wall is entirely taken up by a bookshelf that, along with many dozens of books, hosts exquisite Asian art, including vases and tea sets. The thing about the room that most strikes me is that Michael Spence's wooden desk is empty. There's not a thing on it, not even a pen or computer. A small table adjacent holds an in-tray and various papers, but the main work space is a blank canvas. The airy office feels like a place where one could think uncluttered thoughts.

Michael, a man in his mid-fifties with a warm smile and a soft voice, gestures to a table and some chairs in front of his desk and we sit. He has a cup of tea and after I ask for a glass of water, he starts to tell me his story.

Michael met Beth at Oxford University in 1988, when he was twenty-six and she was twenty-three. They shared a strong Christian faith and spent nearly two decades living and working in the UK, attending church together and building a family. They were very settled in the Oxford community when an offer came in 2008 for Michael to become vice-chancellor at the University of Sydney. The eldest of their five children was sixteen and the youngest was three. Michael and Beth had no great desire to relocate to Australia – Beth was American in fact – but the job was too interesting to resist.

The first sign that something was wrong came about four years after their arrival, when Beth complained of a sore hip. She had always been extremely fit, skilled at rowing, basketball and volleyball; one of those people who never goes to the doctor. Michael and Beth had recently bought a new bed and they blamed that for the hip discomfort. Then, a few weeks later, she became ill with stomach pain as well.

'She was admitted to hospital on November the twenty-eighth, 2012,' Michael says very precisely and deliberately. 'On the third of December she was diagnosed as having cancer in her back, bowel, liver and hips. And by the twenty-second of December, she was dead.'

It is shocking to hear him lay it out like that. It's very hard to comprehend that a healthy young mother of five can be here one month and gone the next. To my mortification, as Michael keeps talking, I start to weep. It's the thought of the smallest of the five children.

'I'm so sorry to cry,' I apologise. 'I'm a terrible sook, I'm so sorry.'

'It's absolutely fine,' Michael says, 'don't worry.'

The reason I'm horrified to cry in front of him is that this is his story and if he can remain composed after enduring such a dreadful thing, then it feels self-indulgent and attention-seeking of me to do otherwise. He's very kind in his response and so I let go of feeling bad and before long I pull myself back together.

'When the doctors broke the news to you on the third of December, what did they say?' I ask.

'The doctors found it very distressing. I'm not a medical professional, but I think, like any professional, they deal with these situations by having patterns at work, like everyone has patterns at work. They're used to people dying after a long battle with cancer, or old people dying of cancer. But a young person dying quickly of cancer is challenging. Beth's oncologist cried when she met Beth,' Michael says. 'Afterwards, more than the usual number of medical professionals asked for counselling support, as they do when they're having trouble at work.'

The other thing that was different for Beth's doctors was that she didn't panic or fall apart or rail against her death. Michael and Beth didn't want what he calls 'hero' interventions. They wanted treatment but not measures to prolong life for the sake of it. On the final day of her life, Beth was not frightened and nor was she in pain.

'When she was about to die, she wanted to take all the tubes off,' Michael tells me. 'The nurse said, "She's very distressed," and I said, "No, she thinks she's going home." Beth opened her eyes and she said three times, "I and the Father are one," which is a line from John. And then she died. We were very lucky. It wasn't a horrible experience.'

'Did you have any sense when you got the diagnosis that it would be over so quickly?' I ask.

'This sounds really hokey, but all through this process and afterwards, there were what I would call moments of grace, moments where I was prepared for what was happening. In the shower, nine months before, in some random moment, I had been thinking, What if Beth died? And I thought about her funeral, and this is where we would have it, how we'd have it; it was such a weird thing to think about. But when it came to organising the funeral, I had thought about it.'

I ask Michael whether, before his wife became ill, anything terrible had happened in his life, beyond the normal, anticipated losses such as the death of his parents.

'No, I had a very benign life,' he says.

'Did you ever think afterwards, So this is how my life has turned out, this is who I am, a widowed father of five?'

Michael thinks for a moment. 'No, you're just so busy surviving, you don't think about those things. I think your view of the world changes, though. My eldest son says the difference for him was getting onto escalators. He said he would think about all the people he passed going the other way: What particular moment of grief or tragedy or disappointment are *you* dealing with at the moment?'

'And what about for you, how do you think your view changed?'

Again Michael pauses to think. 'I kept a list on my phone of ways in which I felt looked after. Bizarre coincidences and things that would happen seemed like God saying, "I haven't altogether forgotten you, I'm still here, we can get through this." I think it deepened my faith. And I don't say that glibly, because I know for lots of people, having a sad experience of one kind or another can really decimate their faith. So I don't say it the slightest bit piously or judgementally. But for me, it did deepen my faith.'

One of the toughest things for Michael and his family was that people were so saddened by the tragedy, they often didn't know what to say. Astoundingly, when his daughter Lucy returned to school, only one person among all the teachers and students asked about the death of her mother. Lucy was hurt and bewildered. Michael raised the lack of support with Lucy's form teacher, who said it was up to Lucy to speak to a counsellor if she wanted to talk about her mother.

'And then we got Lucy's first school report. And it said, "Lucy is an amazing girl who's done incredibly well academically and socially, which is remarkable, given that this term she was in a production of *West Side Story*." Nobody said anything in this whole report about her dead mum! So I went and saw the then principal about it and she was terrific. Since then, the school has really improved its way of handling these situations.'

The school's inability to deal sensitively with the death of a child's parent is undoubtedly partly due to the fact that it's difficult for anybody – individuals or institutions – to know how to act in the face of such a tragic event. Michael himself was very conscious on his own first day back at work at the university that he would have to be the person to make things okay for everybody else. He started meetings by thanking people for coming to Beth's funeral or for writing to him. That way the awkwardness quickly dissipated and others didn't feel the pressure to say or do the 'right' thing. Michael's theory is that people become paralysed because they want to offer something authentic or meaningful and they fear not delivering.

'I remember meeting this friend of my daughter's who was a student here. He said, "Dr Spence, I was very sorry to hear about Mrs Spence." I said, "Thank you very much." He said, "How are you doing?" And I said, "Well, Rupert, it's really hard, obviously, but we're doing okay." He said, "I probably can't, but I just want you to know if I can be of help in any way, please let me know." And I said, "Thanks Rupert, I will." And then we went on to talk about other things. After he went away I thought, I wish everybody was just taught to say, "I'm really sorry to hear about your dead wife." Because often people would say things like they didn't want to bring it up because "I didn't want to remind you of it." And you'd think, Oh yeah, I would have forgotten all about it.'

Michael remarried two years after Beth's death, and has had two more children with his new wife, Jenny. They have had great joy and happiness but it's also been tough at times. Jenny instantly became the mother of five stepchildren, as well as going on to have two babies to manage. As much as they adore each other, there's been a huge amount of adjusting to do for everyone.

'I think what I want to say in your book is that the bad things are hard but sometimes the good things are hard too,' Michael says. 'For me, it's a really important point, that life can be hard in its evidently hard moments, but even things that are really good and really worth doing – and I love my wife to bits, and she me, and we have a strong marriage – they can be hard too.'

'If I'm understanding you, what you're saying is that life is both good and bad simultaneously, is that right? So even as Beth was dying you had beautiful moments together in hospital, and even now that you're happily married again with a wonderful family, there are still moments when things are really tough?'

'Yes,' Michael nods. 'One of the strengths of my tradition is the notion that the world is pretty broken. A lot of the time, life is just hard, and even for people who have a relatively benign life, for a lot of the time, stuff's just hard. And it's okay to say stuff's hard, it doesn't do anyone dishonour. It's alright. It's just giving people space to be human.'

By his 'tradition', Michael means his Christian faith. As with Louisa, I try hard to set aside my judgement about religion when we talk. For some reason, any time somebody tells me that the way they cope with hard times is by trusting that God is in control, I want to follow up with, 'Well, that's what you're *supposed* to say, but what do you *really* think?' But again I try to ignore my scepticism and listen properly. Michael Spence is an extremely intelligent, accomplished, insightful person. If he finds value in Christianity, then surely there are lessons for me to draw from that.

'I don't want any of my questions to sound judgemental, I just want to understand,' I say.

'It's okay, ask what you want,' he encourages me.

'Do you literally believe that God exists?' I ask.

'I literally believe that God exists,' he replies. 'Your question is really "Why do I have a faith?" And the answer is external and internal. External because to me, the Christian account of the world makes more sense than any other account of the world. And I suppose internal because it's true to my lived experience.

It makes sense of the world to me not only in the matter of theory, but also as a matter of my heart and spirit.'

When Michael lost Beth, he became more certain in his beliefs about the way the world works, not less certain. As he points out, others can have the exact opposite experience. They can lose faith in whatever they had previously believed. What I need Michael to do for me is not just share his personal history – I need his objective expertise.

'You run a university,' I say. 'It seems to me that so many academic disciplines, whether maths or science or law, are at heart about our desire to impose order on stuff.'

'Yeah, and that's an interesting question,' Michael answers. 'In science, for example, do we impose order on the universe or do we uncover a particular kind of order in the universe? Why do we talk about the "laws" of physics? It's because we have a sense that we're making discoveries, not constructions.'

'So,' I ask, 'how do I start with all these questions I have – how have scholars answered these questions about fate and chance and blindsides?'

He sits for a while to think. 'There are two dominant ways in which people have dealt with this, broadly speaking. Some philosophies have dealt with it by saying there's a complementarity between life and death, between sickness and health, between the destructive and the creative. So there's this sort of creative and destructive dance, the yin and yang thing, all the rest of it. And there's a certain beauty in that pattern. But as an English author once said, that's fine from a long way off, but close up, it doesn't feel like that.'

'The other way is the kind of Middle Eastern, in particular the Judaeo-Christian, way of doing it, of saying, actually somehow health and beauty and life are more authentic, more true, more real, than sickness and death and the rest of it. So then you have to have some sort of explanation as to why the bad things are an aberration.'

Michael tells me about a course at Yale University called A Life Worth Living, which introduces students to speakers from all sorts of different faiths. They hear from committed secular atheists, Marxists, Christians, Muslims, Buddhists. Each speaker answers a series of the same questions: How do you explain suffering? Does death have meaning? What are the characteristics of something you would regard as good?

'There are huge resources in every tradition,' Michael says. 'The thing is, there's no neutral ground. Living a reflective life seems to involve adopting a position in relation to these things and then trying to live coherently within that position.'

We chat about the various psychological and evolutionary theories I've been reading about.

'There seems to be this universal human need to try to find a way to explain why things happen,' I say, 'including why awful things happen.'

'Yes,' he agrees, 'and the interesting meta-question is, Why do we have that need? It is a plausible explanation to say that that need has an evolutionary function, in just keeping us going. But the problem, to me, is that's not how it feels, that's not my lived experience. I want to actually say that, in a deep sense, when I see images of a child who's suffered, or a great disaster, that it is wrong. There is a story in John's Gospel of Jesus at the tomb of Lazarus, where Jesus is angry and weeps, and also a story of Jesus at another place where he meets a man who is unwell, and the verb that's used in the Greek is the same one used for the snorting of an angry horse. There's this notion that it's okay, and indeed right, to say that things shouldn't be like this. To me, they're pretty powerful stories. I suppose when I've had a hard time one way or another, that's been very important.'

With that answer, Michael helps something click in my brain. Scientific explanations are only the background to the story I'm interested in. Evolutionary biology is an important way of understanding why humans feel the way they do, but it's how that wiring connects in every individual that really interests me. If Louisa believes that being a hostage and having MS made her stronger, or if Michael feels that the death of his wife strengthened his faith, their stories are just as valid when it comes to understanding humanity as theoretical research is. Michael himself suggests that I take an anecdotal approach, using academic papers for context.

'I think that's a really interesting exercise, and then think about what are the commonalities of experience,' he suggests. 'And how do you deal with it from within? You can try to see the world through the eyes of a particular person.'

Meeting Michael frees me from feeling that answers are sitting out there somewhere in the universe, waiting for me to find them. I will find some insights in the books and journals that Cathy is sending my way, but I can still use my journalistic skills too. There is going to be enormous wisdom and insight in the lived experience of others.

Two

We're All in This Together

The big news stories that happened when I was a young reporter in the 1990s seem far more memorable to me than recent headlines, perhaps because the job was still so new and exciting. I vividly recall the days when Princess Diana and INXS frontman Michael Hutchence died, the night that Paul Keating lost the Australian prime ministership, and the scramble to get reporters to Thredbo to cover an enormous landslide. The newsroom bristled with energy as journalists scurried in every direction, phones ringing nonstop. The whiteboard behind the chief of staff's desk, showing the assigning of crews and journalists, was an incomprehensible wall of arrows, lines, names and numbers by the time the evening news bulletin somehow made it to air.

I remember a very famous news photograph taken during one of those intense periods. It's almost as memorable in Australia as the image of accused murderer Lindy Chamberlain unfurling a poster of baby Azaria. It is a picture of a man in a suit, dark hair neatly combed, leaving a church. He clutches three irises, and a bright pink hair elastic is wrapped around one wrist. His eyes are cast downward, face contorted in grief as he weeps uncontrollably. A man on either side grips his arms, holding him upright. One of them is crying and the other looks desperately grim, as they half escort, half carry the stricken man from the church.

The man in the photograph is Walter Mikac, and he's leaving a memorial for the thirty-five victims of the 1996 Port Arthur shooting. Port Arthur was the worst massacre in Australian history, outside colonial times, and it prompted a controversial overhaul of the nation's weapons laws.

Walter would have given anything to not be in that famous picture or thrust into the national spotlight. On 28 April that year, he was playing a round of golf while his wife, Nanette, and two daughters, Alannah and Madeline, aged six and three, were enjoying an outing at the Port Arthur historic site. The trio heard gunfire and were attempting to flee when a car pulled over alongside them. No doubt thinking it was somebody who could help, Nanette walked towards it. The gunman stepped out and fatally shot her and then the two girls.

Like Louisa Hope, Walter Mikac knows there's no comfort in the generalisations of probability if you happen to be the one in the equation. The odds of living in rural Australia, as the Mikac family did in 1996, and being the victim of a gun massacre would have been utterly unlikely. Losing your entire family in such a way would have been a more remote prospect still. Yet that is what happened to Walter, a pharmacist who was at the time in his early thirties.

That devastating experience turned Walter Mikac into one of the most famous faces of tragedy in Australia. It's a group nobody would ever want to join, and yet once you're a member, the public never allows you to leave: Bruce and Denise Morcombe, Lindy Chamberlain, Stuart Diver. In 2008, newspapers ran a story about the death of Garry Lynch, the father of Anita Cobby, one of the most famous murder victims in Australian history. Garry was ninety. Even in death, his life was still defined by the brutal crime visited upon his daughter.

If, like Walter Mikac and those others, you have the great misfortune to find yourself in the middle of a public tragedy that grabs and violently shakes the community, there will never be a time when your life is truly your own again, no matter how many years pass. There will be anniversaries when journalists come knocking, there will be similar tragedies on which you're asked to comment, there will be pressure to 'make a difference', there will be 'Where Are They Now?' magazine articles. The media gives these stories such prominence that we almost come to feel as if we know the people involved. We become emotionally invested in finding out what happens to them next.

There's another reason why we become fascinated with these people's lives. As the last chapter explained, we are very rattled by major events that shatter our sense of security. Our minds keep turning them over until we find ways to make sense of what happened. The more shocking and awful the tragedy, the harder it is for us to process. Our individual brains behave predictably in that quest, but we also act predictably as a community. Any news story of a disaster will be followed by more news stories of the collective reaction. We almost always leave flowers and create memorials and gather together.

I've seen this pattern of group mourning repeated time and time again during my journalism career but now I want to understand why we do it. What exactly is the community looking for in the aftermath of a major tragedy, and why does it act the way it does? What does that behaviour tell us about ourselves? And how does the way the rest of us act affect the already shattered people at the centre of the storm?

One night a few months after the twentieth anniversary of the Port Arthur massacre, I'm sitting in a pub on the northern coast of New South Wales waiting to meet Walter Mikac for dinner. It's a rainy night and I watch for him out the window. Frankly, I'm scared to meet him. What happened to Walter is close to the worst thing I could ever imagine happening to me. I'm worried I will start to cry when he talks about it, as I did with Michael Spence, or that my face will betray my fear. I'm conscious that so many people over the years will have treated Walter like That Port Arthur Guy, not as a normal man to whom a terrible thing happened. I'm so nervous that I've pre-gamed my small talk as if

I'm on a date. (I've read that he likes gardening, so I have a few anecdotes about my plants, and I figure he probably likes AFL because he's originally from Melbourne.)

As I fidget with my cutlery, I see Walter park his car in the street and cross the road. He's wearing a light grey hoodie over a business shirt and looks much as he did twenty years ago, perhaps with a little less hair on top, a tiny bit heavier. He's still a handsome man.

After we shake hands, I blather through my prepared ice-breakers, praying I don't appear as giant a goose as I feel, and we order our meals (Moreton Bay bugs for Walter, a rib-eye for me). My fears prove unfounded: Walter is easy to talk to and my nerves dissolve very quickly.

It turns out I'm far from the first person to fear talking to him. In the year after the massacre, Walter would go shopping and women would sometimes recognise him, burst into tears and quickly rush away without saying a word. The horror of what had happened to him was so unfathomable that even close friends fled.

'The one I think about,' he tells me, 'was my friend Doug, who I played cricket with and who was the dad of the girl who worked in my pharmacy. And one day, I was walking down the street and he was coming the other way. As soon as he saw me he turned and started walking the other way. I sort of had to make a split-second decision. What am I going to do? If I let him go, we'll probably never have a conversation ever again. So I started walking quicker. As I started walking quicker, he was nearly running. I caught up to him and put my hand on his shoulder and as he turned around, he just had tears streaming down his face. I said, "It's okay, Doug, you don't have to say anything."'

I can completely understand why Doug would do that, and yet at the same time it seems so terrible that Walter, in the midst of all his anguish, was the one who had to console others. It reminds me of Michael Spence accepting that he would have to be the one to diffuse any awkwardness at work, even though he was the person suffering the most. Walter says that having friends avoid him for fear of not knowing what to say or do was one of the worst things in the aftermath of losing his family.

'If you thought someone was genuinely a good friend, and you had shared a lot of experience with them, and they avoided you, that hurt,' Walter says. 'You could sort of understand, but by the same token, it's another part of loss. You've lost whatever you had but then people just go by the wayside and it's more loss. There's nothing anyone could say, no matter how badly it came out, that could be as bad as what's already happened to you. So it's much better for people to just let you know that they're there to help, if you need it. For people to show that they're still there is the most important thing.'

While some of Walter's friends weren't up to that task, he found that the insensitivity of strangers could be appalling too. There was a combination of intense curiosity and fear.

'You're conscious that people are looking at you or maybe making judgements about how you're going. That's a hard thing because you can't be sad every minute of the day,' he says. 'But sometimes I'd go out with my brothers, who were single at the time, to nightclubs in Melbourne and people would see you laughing or joking and dancing around the dance floor. People would actually say, "So you're over it?" or, "You're better now?" and I would say, "It's just a distraction, it's a way of passing time."'

Walter tells me he felt like he was living in a fishbowl.

'People would come up and say, "Aren't you that guy that had all your family killed in Port Arthur?" without any other part to it. That happened for quite a while. People would just say it without really thinking. People see your car somewhere and they make assumptions. There were a few times where people thought I was sleeping in the pharmacy and that I wasn't coping,' he recalls.

What Walter is implying, but doesn't say directly, is that people were wondering if he would kill himself. When they speculated about that, what they were really grappling with was the question of whether or not they would kill themselves in his position. So I ask him what might seem a shockingly direct question, because I think I would be wasting his time – as well as that of everyone interviewed for this book and your time as a reader – if I didn't ask the questions everybody secretly thinks about.

'Nobody has more knowledge of or access to the means to commit suicide than a pharmacist,' I say. 'What made you think that life was worth carrying on?'

I'm glad that Walter doesn't seem remotely offended.

'The thing that kept coming up for me was family,' he replies. 'My thought was, All these people have battled really hard. They're hurting as well because it's their grandchildren, or their nieces.

It was a sense that I really can't do it. There's been enough hurt here. It's not to say that I haven't thought of wanting to do that, but it would have to be really bad for that to be the case. I kept holding onto the hope that whilst today or this week was awful – the court case was on and it was going to be very traumatic – that once that was over, there's hope that the next week I might go away and build new memories or share things with other people, and that would be good.'

There were even times, I learn, amidst his terrible suffering when Walter felt fortunate.

'There was a lady I visited, Carol Loughton, who was in the café and lost her daughter,' he recalls.

Carolyn Loughton had been in the Broad Arrow Café, one of the bloodiest sites of the massacre. She suffered terrible physical injuries from gunshot and was also left with great psychological scars because her daughter was killed in front of her.

'Whenever I went to see Carol, I actually felt lucky. I thought, You've lost Nanette and the children. But at least you haven't been physically hurt. If you can muster up the energy, you can do anything from here,' Walter says.

It wasn't as if mustering up the energy was easy. At times it was near impossible. Yet while some strangers and friends were insensitive, the community also came together in ways that were extraordinary. In the weeks immediately following the massacre, there was a nonstop delivery of food to Walter's house. There was also an astounding number of letters, around three thousand, from people all over the world. There were presents too: soft toys, religious material, cheques for large sums of money. The Pharmacy Guild of Australia was particularly generous, organising a roster of pharmacists from all over the country to keep Walter's small business running while he took time out to grieve.

'It was pretty humbling,' he says. 'It was a case of there's a lot more good people in the world than bad. That did help restore my faith in humanity.'

Another way in which the community helped was by plugging Walter into a network of men who had lost children in the Dunblane school massacre in Scotland. (Around the same time as Port Arthur, a gunman killed sixteen children and a teacher in one of the worst mass murders in UK history.) Some of the fathers visited Australia and Walter formed a bond with them. Then he and his brother went to Scotland and met the families again.

'Prior to that, I was thinking, There's nobody in the world who really knows how I feel. Being in their company was a really healing thing. For them to be able to share, for me to be able to share, to have tears, to be able to talk about things that you can't necessarily talk to your family about because it's either too gruesome or they're just dark thoughts. You don't want to burden people with them.'

When Walter now sees tragedy befall others he watches them start on the same journey he once took: the shock, the grief, the media intrusion, the community reaction, the struggle to keep going. He feels a connection with such people.

'I read this article a month ago, in *Good Weekend*, about a man named Matt Golinski,' Walter says. (Matt Golinski is a chef who was severely burned in a house fire on the Sunshine Coast in Queensland while trying to rescue his wife and three daughters, all of whom died.) 'I tore the article out. I subscribed to his website, hoping if he saw my name he might contact me. I would love to have a conversation with him, just to say things aren't the same but there is some light.'

It touches me greatly that Walter, such a gentle soul, did not directly contact Matt Golinski, but instead reached out so subtly. There's no doubt that twenty years after losing his family, Walter has much wisdom to share. He has managed to rebuild his life. He remarried and has a daughter. He lives by the beach and tries to go for a swim every day. He owns a pharmacy that he shares with a business partner, so he works one week on, one week off. Quite a few people in his local community don't even know his history. He's just Walter the chemist.

'Twenty years on, what does grief feel like compared to what it felt like one year on?' I ask.

'A year on, you're just functioning. I really didn't have any idea what I was going to do in the future. Twenty years on, it's probably more like a surgical wound. You can see the scar. You've experienced a whole gamut of emotions but it sits okay. I still think about what the children would have been doing at this age. They might have finished uni. It's a daily thought, just the loss of potential and what they could have been. Sometimes, I just wish so much that I could give them a hug.'

His simple need to hug his little girls is the one part of our interview that nearly undoes me, and I can see Walter is immensely sad too.

'Do the questions ever stop about why this happened to you?' I ask in a wobbly voice. 'How do you stop asking yourself that?'

'You try. I still do. Things like if I hadn't taken the car they wouldn't have been there [trying to leave Port Arthur on foot, and therefore more vulnerable to gunfire], and that's probably true. Those things keep going, they still occasionally go around through your head. But I think once you gain an acceptance that they're not coming back, you can ask those questions without it flooring you,' he says.

I ask whether he's scared about other people he loves dying, about experiencing more pain.

'I personally don't feel scared about dying,' Walter says. 'I suppose when you've seen it that close, it's just inevitable, but I do cherish the time. I want to spoil my mum and do things because that opportunity won't always be there. The number one lesson that comes out of what happened to me is that you don't know when things are going to change. Life is not promised today or tomorrow. It can all be gone.'

After he lost his family, Walter wanted to stay connected with other people rather than retreat from the community, even though in some ways it had added to his pain. He had a strong desire to find a way to honour the memories of Nanette, Alannah and Madeline. His first thought was to take advantage of his unwanted public profile to support the Australian government's campaign to reform national gun laws. When it came to dealing with the media, Walter remembers initially feeling vulnerable, gullible and exploited. After a while, he figured out how to set limits and turn interviews towards issues on which he wanted to focus. Then once the gun laws had been reformed, he established the Alannah & Madeline Foundation to help children who are the victims of violence.

'The one thing I promised myself and Nanette and the kids was that if they weren't here, I wanted to make the best of what I could for them. To see the Alannah & Madeline Foundation, to see all the incredible things we've been able to do to help other children, it's phenomenal,' Walter says.

'Everyone still knows their names. They're still there,' I offer.

'It's helped me a lot more than I think I even realise. Knowing they're remembered in a good, positive way and that it's going to continue beyond my lifetime. That makes it even more gratifying and special.'

The night before we met, I had a nightmare in which Walter came to my house. He was in a wheelchair, his body slumped and broken as if he had a degenerative disease. Even his teeth were yellowed and decaying. It was as if my subconscious could not fathom that somebody who had suffered as much as Walter would bear no outward marks of it. Meeting him has helped disavow me of the fear that there are some things which prevent a person carrying on.

Somehow people do keep going after such devastation. It's clear that sharing your experience with people who understand it helps, and so does finding a purpose. Walter still carries deep pain but he's no longer that barely functioning man you might remember from the news, holding the irises outside the church. He has a good, meaningful life and he finds happiness in all parts of it. By the time we say goodnight outside the pub,

I feel comforted to have learned that even though he's suffered the cruellest blow life could inflict, Walter Mikac has endured.

When the community learns of a tragedy like Walter's, the thought, That could have been me, is quickly replaced by: If that happened to me, I could never survive. It's an example of the tendency to think of ourselves as exceptional: Walter might have handled the loss of his entire family but I wouldn't. One of the reasons that somebody like Walter becomes an unwitting celebrity is that the community is morbidly fascinated to see how people cope with something that they couldn't personally imagine enduring. It's a way of letting our brains wrestle with one of life's most challenging truths – that things can change catastrophically in an instant – without having to suffer it ourselves. As Walter learned from his painful encounters with both friends and strangers, many people can't stand getting too close to that reality.

The ripple effect of a national tragedy like Port Arthur is immense. It spreads outwards from the victims to the first responders, to families and friends and to people who live locally. Then the wave crashes over the rest of us as we watch the horror on television. Along with despair and a sense of helplessness, we experience collective trauma, because the values that underpin our community's safe operation – trust in each other, public security, reliable routine – have been torn apart. We are desperate to stitch things back together again as quickly as possible.

This compulsion to get 'back to normal' causes communities to behave in foreseeable patterns, just as our individual brains react predictably to awful events. Two collective behaviours in particular attend every tragedy: an effort to bond with one another, and a drive to build something positive from what's happened.

The need to connect with other people after loss is almost culturally universal. One of the most common ways Western communities do this is through spontaneous memorials of flowers, cards, candles or toys. After the death of Princess Diana, more than 50 million bouquets were laid outside Buckingham Palace, and after the 1999 Columbine High School massacre in the US, authorities eventually removed more than two hundred thousand memorial items from the scene.

People act in this way because sharing grief helps them find solidarity and meaning. The compulsion to visit make-shift memorials is so strong that the volume of visitors can pose problems for public safety. Governments and police always try to manage grieving crowds rather than disperse them because community recovery is innately tied to the free and collective expression of grief. It is a time of extreme brittleness and any attempt to block spontaneous memorials can transform mass grieving into something angry or toxic. If they're handled well, such sites instead become places of strength and support.

Following the Lindt Café siege, a vast field of flowers soon blanketed Sydney's Martin Place. A few nights after the tragedy, I was at a work function nearby that ended late. Close to midnight, I visited the memorial myself. I'm not sure why: curiosity, perhaps, or the need for reassurance that things would be okay. My lasting memory is of the overwhelming floral scent on the velvety night air. Even at that hour, many people still lingered. I was surprised to find that visiting the site truly was comforting. It gave me the sense that kindness and unity would triumph over destruction. It was almost as if you could see the communal fabric being sewn back together.

Nobody understands you as well as somebody who has been through the same things, as Walter Mikac learned when he spent time with the Dunblane fathers. Emotional bonding can aid recovery, and this idea has underpinned the concept of support groups for decades. Alcoholics Anonymous is the best known of them, but today you can find groups for everything from victims of crime to parents of children with cancer.

Thanks to the internet, you don't even have to attend a support group face to face. There are hundreds of thousands of online groups worldwide, offering support on everything imaginable. Children of Alzheimer's sufferers can connect with each other, and even people with severe dental anxiety have their own network. Online support groups usually don't have a trained professional steering them but they offer some benefits that face-to-face interactions don't. Anonymity permits people to speak without inhibition. Writing things in a forum or Facebook post can also help process feelings. In both the digital and real worlds, participation can help restore a sense of control, wellbeing and self-confidence. Some group members take comfort from giving support as well as receiving it.

Closely tied to the community's desire to bond is the drive to see something positive come from tragedy. This may take the form of demands for formal inquiries or changes to the law so that similar tragedies can be avoided. The gun law reform that occurred after Port Arthur is one example. Sometimes people who share experiences of tragedy work together to build charitable organisations, many of which, whether for multiple sclerosis or lung cancer, rely heavily for volunteers and fundraising on those who've been personally affected. A 2017 Australian study asked people who donated to health or medical research why they did so. A whopping 87 per cent replied that they, a friend or a family member had been affected by the condition. A broader study – conducted the previous year and which looked at philanthropy across all sectors, not just health – reported that two-thirds of donations came from people who had a friend or family member linked to the cause.

Unfortunately, being part of a community is not all upside when tragedy strikes. As Walter Mikac learned, the fishbowl effect and the insensitivity of strangers can wound deeply. Those of us a step removed from the catastrophe are not immune to damage either, if we absorb too much of it through the media. Numerous studies, including after the 1990 Gulf War, the 1995 Oklahoma City bombing, the September 2001 terrorist attacks, the 2012 Sandy Hook Elementary School massacre, and the 2013 Boston Marathon bombing, show that constant media exposure to awful events harms the mental health of a community. Simply by repeatedly viewing footage of disasters, any one of us can end up experiencing some of the same symptoms of post-traumatic stress as people more closely tied to the event. In the post-9/11 world, images of terrorist attacks are even more confronting, thanks to witnesses sharing real-time, unedited footage via social media.

While tens of thousands of people were directly affected by 9/11, the collective trauma was felt much wider. Millions of people around the globe saw the distressing and pervasive television images of the terrorist attacks, many of which aired live. We watched the second passenger jet smash into the World Trade Center as it happened. We saw people diving from the burning tower, suiciding rather than waiting to die. We watched bleeding, dazed people stumbling and staggering through dust and rubble on the streets of New York, trying to get to safety. I'm sure I'm not alone in vividly recalling where I was as I watched those images, fear curdling in my gut about what would happen next. Was the Eiffel Tower about to blow up? Were Australian planes about to slam into the Sydney Harbour Bridge? It felt as if my entire world was tilting, even though I was on the other side of the planet.

The research into television exposure to 9/11 is particularly comprehensive. A study that started in 2001 looked at the mental health of 931 Americans before the terrorist attacks and then for the two years afterwards (it tried to equalise for pre-existing mental conditions). The majority of the sample was not directly exposed to the attacks but watched them on live TV or soon after. Four out of five respondents reported symptoms including distress and heightened feelings of vulnerability, and many of those symptoms remained elevated in the weeks and months after 9/11. The compulsion among the sample group to find some sort of meaning in what had happened was similar to the behaviour observed in studies of people personally recovering from incest and sudden bereavement.

Research after the Boston Marathon bombing found something similar. On 15 April 2013, at the finish line of the famous race, terrorists detonated two homemade bombs, killing three people and injuring several hundred others. It was the first major terrorist attack in the US since 9/11. Reporters and spectators filmed the mayhem on their smart phones and graphic images were widely shared. Researchers found that the more frequently that people with close connections to the disaster watched coverage of it, the more they experienced psychological distress and health problems. That's unsurprising; what's more notable is evidence of the same thing in people without direct links to the tragedy. Both real-life exposure and video-exposure were found to be associated with post-traumatic stress symptoms, including flashbacks (uncontrollably replaying in your mind what you've seen) and fear conditioning (a learned fear of activities associated with the trauma, such as being in a large crowd).

The good news is that communities are generally very resilient. The number of people who feel *acute* stress is low and recovery is fast. Most of us are able to adapt, adjust and move on after a period of short-term distress. There are certain factors that can help us do that more effectively. We need to see that somebody in authority has taken control of the situation. We need the space to bond together, and we need to be shepherded towards ways to make something good come from something bad. We need to hear words that describe how we are feeling and to reassure us that things will be okay. In other words, we need strong leaders. During major tragedies, that role frequently falls to politicians.

If good leaders put those things in place, the community will find itself on a path to recovery. It is a tough, high-stakes job for those who find themselves in leadership at such times, because the public is particularly attentive and also volatile. What equips a person to speak to an entire nation at a time of extraordinary community tragedy? How do they know what to say and what to do? And where do they find the strength to do it, when they are probably as rattled as the rest of us?

As I watched a ceremony to mark the twentieth anniversary of the Port Arthur massacre, the possible answers to these questions came to me in the form of an elderly white-haired man in a black trench coat, walking a little stiffly among the mourners.

The former Australian prime minister John Howard was the only person formally invited to attend the Port Arthur service, a mark of gratitude and respect for his national leadership at the time. Against tough opposition inside his own political party, he reformed Australia's gun laws, working alongside campaigners such as Walter Mikac to ensure that a massacre on the scale of Port Arthur could never recur in Australia. (Walter himself did not attend the twentieth anniversary event, instead keeping his own commemoration private after so much public attention over the years.)

John Howard dealt with more Australian loss of life during his term in office than any other Australian prime minister outside of wartime. That's partly to do with his longevity in the job, as the nation's second-longest-serving PM (1996–2007), and partly because there was an unusual series of mass-fatality events during his tenure. His first two years in the Lodge were particularly notable for the range and scale of disaster. As well as Port Arthur and its thirty-five deaths, there was the crash of a Black Hawk helicopter in Townsville that killed eighteen soldiers, and the Thredbo landslide, which also claimed eighteen lives. Howard was PM during 9/11 (eleven Australians were killed) and the 2002 Bali bombings (eighty-eight Australian deaths). There were numerous other smaller-scale tragedies too.

When John Howard and I meet for tea one day in his office, high in a skyscraper with views over Sydney Harbour, I ask him what he considered the role of prime minister to be at such times.

'You had to put what happened into some sort of national context,' he says. 'That varied according to the incident. It really depended on whether there was a national significance or something about the tragedy that required a change of public attitude or public policy.'

When John Howard first became prime minister, the media had only recently begun its transition to the 24-hour news cycle. CNN had started doing this in the US in 1980, but it was that network's round-the-clock coverage of the 1991 Iraq War, live from Baghdad, that transformed the news business. It changed viewers' expectations about what they could see on television and it altered networks' ideas about the product they had to deliver. Sky News in Australia adopted similar coverage in 1996, a month before Howard's election: it was the first, and for many years the sole, dedicated news channel in Australia.

During Howard's term in office, the ABC and commercial television news operations added more bulletins throughout the day, in addition to the flagship evening broadcasts watched by millions of Australians. Newspapers would soon begin publishing their content online as events happened, rather than just once a day. The constant need to fill space meant that the media's appetite for content became relentless. New information and pictures were required nonstop to keep stories turning over and to inspire consumers to keep watching or clicking. That in turn changed the way politicians engaged with the media. They responded to demand for commentary and also saw opportunities to fill the vacuum with their agendas.

John Howard was the first person to lead the nation during this new media era. Politicians had always been expected to rally the nation at times of crisis, but the impact of disasters and tragedies on the community at large was now magnified. Networks would slip into rolling coverage for major stories, such as the Thredbo landslide or the death of Princess Diana or 9/11. Political leaders were expected to offer commentary. In the 1980s, Bob Hawke wasn't asked for constant observations about the disappearance of Azaria Chamberlain. Malcolm Fraser didn't have to muster a profound reflection on the death of John Lennon. If those news stories had happened today, though, the prime minister would unquestionably be expected to have something to say. And it's not only to fill air time, it's also because many viewers want leaders to help them make sense of what they're seeing.

'People are looking for somebody to verbalise how they're feeling,' Howard says. 'You've got to try and find the right words. That's not easy.'

Howard often emphasised heroism, family and mateship. To him, those things are the core of what it means to be Australian and he tried to help people by bonding them through national identity. Many of his press conferences were accompanied by displays of the flag, and the national anthem was played at public memorials. Howard's approach seemed to be to try to unite the community as one Australian family, with himself in the role of reassuring father.

He often spoke off the cuff and from the heart. His remarks after the 2002 Bali bombings, in the Great Hall at Parliament House on 24 October, were typical of the way he would seek to comfort Australians:

. . . this event has told us something of our nation. It has reminded us of things that we knew and understood about our nature and our character as a people. It has reminded us of the great verity of Australian life that in crisis we are all mates together. The sense of mateship that ensured that within 48 hours the injured were evacuated back to Australia and the support mechanisms that have been delivered to people in the days that have followed the tragedy have reminded us of that great trait of the Australian character.

The other great characteristic of which we have been reminded is our sense of defiance. We will not be deterred from living our lives. The young of Australia will not be

deterred from travelling in the years ahead. We will not for-
sake the values of this nation which mark it with great respect
around the world. We will continue to live the kind of lives
that we regard as the birthright of all Australians. And we've
also been reminded of the great tolerance of the Australian
people. The Australian people, deeply angered and grieved as
they are, are not about to abandon the spirit of openness and
tolerance which is also one of our great hallmarks.

During Howard's prime ministership, journalists observed
that not only was he adept at knowing what to say, but he also
perfectly judged the right notes of restraint and sincerity during
times of national tragedy. Canberra press gallery journalist Misha Schubert wrote in *The Age*: 'The unlikely sight of a
buttoned-up politician throwing his arms around beefy bikies
and dreadlocked young women can make you double-take. But
his gestures are often spot on in times of pain and loss.'

Howard's air of awkward authenticity caused many voters to
respond favourably, usually handing him improved poll numbers
straight after national disasters. Following Port Arthur, his
approval rating hit 67 per cent. After September 11, he was at
61 per cent and after the 2004 South Asian tsunami, 63 per cent.
Few politicians ever see such heady numbers, let alone after eight
years in office. These bumps in his rating after crises caused his
political opponents to snipe that he was a master at milking
tragedy for political gain.

I read aloud one such comment to Howard, made by his
nemesis and predecessor, Paul Keating: '[Howard] always pops

up at these occasions – he's at every national, international catastrophe, sort of representative of White Lady Funerals. He's made an art form out of sadness and sorrow.'

'He said that, did he? He must have been feeling particularly ignored,' sniffs Howard. 'Did I ever think I was conscious of that? Never. I never wanted to be accused of ever milking something like that. I was conscious not to overdo it. But I was also conscious you were expected to say things.'

'There was no option to not say anything?' I ask.

'No. The important thing was to find the right words to say it.'

'I noticed when I looked at some of your remarks after these things that you would often pull it back to talking about family. Why?'

'That's what people identify with most in their lives and whenever there's something like this, you have a sense of vulnerability of your own family.'

'Did you?'

'Yes. But human nature is such that you can't allow that to play too heavily on your mind. Otherwise, you become immobilised.'

In John Howard's personal life, there was nothing that had prepared him to assume the role of mourner-in-chief. To use Michael Spence's description, his life experiences had been 'benign'. Howard had no professional background or training in psychology, medicine, trauma or bereavement. He was fifty-six years old when he became prime minister, and most fortunately he had experienced only the anticipated losses of life, such as the deaths of his parents. His three children were healthy and he had enjoyed good luck (and made sound choices) with his marriage and his career. Even when things occasionally seemed like they were not going his way, they actually were. In 1968, Howard missed out on winning the state seat of Drummoyne in the New South Wales parliament by just 420 votes. If he hadn't suffered that blow, he wouldn't have been free to run for the federal seat of Bennelong in 1974 and most likely would never have become prime minister. The only slight hitch in Howard's life was that he had a hearing problem in one ear, although fortune even favoured him there – advances in technology during his lifetime meant it was of little impediment.

The one thing that Howard believes did perhaps help him intuit how to respond to trauma was his many years of experience as a member of parliament before becoming prime minister.

'People would often come and talk to you about things. Not normally come and talk to me as the local member about the tragedy, but the discussion would often morph into that. I had a number of examples of parents who came to talk to me about the circumstances of their children's suicide,' he recollects.

Early in his term as prime minister, he was also, for the first time in his life, dealt a potentially life-changing blow: his beloved wife Janette was diagnosed with ovarian cancer. It was kept secret from the public at the time but it shook the Howards to the core. It undoubtedly gave him some additional insight into human vulnerability.

'We as a family confronted that in a very open way. We talked to our children. We did all we could to share. We were both very realistic about it,' he recalls. 'Janette said, "Look we've just got to keep going and hope." She said to me at the time it had a big effect on her, thinking more about her priorities.'

'What about for you?' I ask.

'It was a reminder of the fragility of life and I was very grateful for that. I think for both of us, having the demands of the new job probably helped. She didn't go to things with me, obviously, for several months. Fortunately, she had a good surgeon and we worried about a possible return but it hasn't happened. More than twenty years now. She's very fortunate.'

Howard's limited personal and professional experience of grief meant he had to learn quickly on the job. The people he met who were going through terrible tragedy may have been strangers to him, but to many of them, the prime minister felt like somebody they knew.

'The very important thing is that the last thing a prime minister or anybody in a position like public office should do is be diffident or hesitant. You're only magnifying their grief when you're meant to be there to help them, not to add to their problems,' he says firmly.

'Did you feel the need to be strong and not to cry?' I ask.

'I think you owed it to them to recognise it was their emotions that had to be on display. You had to be sensitive – if you couldn't talk or offer some kind of physical comfort, you're not much help to them. I didn't mind people crying in my arms, and that happened a lot. I encouraged them in a sense to do so. It's their sadness that really matters. You've got to try to help them with that.'

One of the political skills for which Howard was most noted was his ability to read the collective mood of the Australian people. His admirers would say he stayed ahead of it; his detractors would say he manipulated it. Most of what he tells me about how his gut led him to act aligns perfectly with what professionals recommend. He always tried to meet the bereaved person at their response, not with something preconceived.

'One of the things I was very conscious of was that different people expect different things in those circumstances. Some of them want a hug, some of them want a handshake. Some of them just want to talk to you, it depends on their personalities.'

'How did you judge that?' I ask.

'You just make your own judgement,' Howard says, in that firm way (his opponents would say 'stubborn') that he has. 'I remember spending a lot of time with the people who had lost family members in the Bali attack and they really wanted to talk about it, talk about what had happened and some of the movements their children might have had just before they were killed.'

It's obvious that the more lives lost in a tragedy, the more it becomes a defining moment in the national consciousness. I also want John Howard's opinion about why the death of one individual sometimes snowballs into something huge in the community. An example is eighteen-year-old Sydney boy, Thomas Kelly, who was killed by a stranger's punch on the streets of Kings Cross in 2012. The case sparked New South Wales' controversial 'lock out laws', under which pubs and clubs had to close their doors at 1.30 am and serve last drinks at 3 am.

Phillip Hughes' freak accident is another example. Hughes was not a household name when he was killed by a cricket ball hitting the precise spot on his head not covered by his helmet, and his death had no implications for public policy. Yet it stopped the nation.

'I think it's a combination of the extent to which the death and the circumstances of it find a ready identification in the minds of people in the community. I think another part of it is if the circumstances are blindingly unjust. You take Thomas Kelly, seems a perfectly nice kid out on his first date, sort of singing, holding hands with a girl as they walk down the street. The next minute, he's dead. Parents seeing that react,' says Howard. 'People doing a perfectly normal thing, not doing anything wrong, and then out of the blue something like that happens. That has a big impact on people. Phillip Hughes, it was just such a freak accident.'

John Howard remains acutely conscious that some of his own decisions directly led to the deaths of Australians. His call to involve Australia in the US-led wars in Afghanistan and Iraq ultimately resulted in the deaths of forty-four Australian soldiers and ongoing suffering for their families.

'One of the things I've done since I've been out of office, I've written every time there was a soldier killed in Afghanistan. I'd send a handwritten note to the parents or wives or other loved ones. I suppose because I sent them there,' he says.

'Is it a heavy weight to carry, the knowledge that people have died because you made decisions?'

'Yes. You don't do it lightly. I thought all the decisions I took were correct. I don't regret the decisions, but I do feel the sense of responsibility.'

John Howard is, at the time of writing, close to eighty years old. As the marvellous Australian author Helen Garner once wrote of herself, he possesses a lengthening past and a shortening future. He is not an especially reflective man, not prone to musing over paths untravelled or words unsaid, and yet it can't escape him that his own life is in its twilight.

'Do you think about your own death?' I ask, slightly mortified at my own gall.

'Yes. I have the normal intimations of mortality,' he says.

'Are you scared of it?'

'No. Nothing I can do about it,' he replies, the most Howard-esque of answers imaginable.

I'm struck again that, in contrast to all the heartbreak Howard saw firsthand as prime minister, his own life has been remarkably sunny. He has managed to get through his almost eighty years not only virtually unscathed, but amassing some of the greatest treasures life can offer – health, family, happiness, career success, financial security, interesting experiences.

'When you look back over your life, it has been amazing; you've had a lot of good fortune,' I suggest.

'An enormous amount of fortune,' he agrees.

'Do you think it was fate? Was it God's plan for you? Or was it luck, dumb chance?'

Howard thinks for a moment. 'It's a combination of persistence, some ability, good fortune. Perhaps an understanding of the character of the Australian people that was better than

average for people in politics. I had a very stable family upbringing. I've been incredibly lucky with Janette and my three children,
I think that is my happiest achievement,' he says.

I begin to gather my things and make moves to leave.

'Sure, I've been lucky. In a few things, I was unlucky. I wasn't
as good a cricketer as I'd liked to have been,' he laughs.

'In the greater scheme of things, a small sacrifice?'

'A very small sacrifice, yes,' the former prime minister agrees
jovially as we shake hands and go our separate ways.

Three

The Eye of the Storm

While you've been reading this book, you've been putting your trust in me as a journalist, and to continue reading, you must believe that I've been telling the truth about what Louisa Hope, Michael Spence, Walter Mikac and John Howard said to me. You must trust that my reporting of their remarks is accurate, and that the parts of their stories I've chosen to emphasise have been fair and reasonable. You don't have to agree with my interpretations or conclusions, but as my reader you are relying on me to steer you soundly so that you can form your own judgements.

Wielding that kind of influence is humbling for an author, but it's particularly serious for a journalist reporting a live national tragedy. Then, the information shared and the conclusions drawn can literally become matters of life and death, for people who may need to decide, for example, whether to evacuate during a natural disaster. The trust the community puts in the media at such times is extraordinary.

It's impossible to fully understand how we react to catastrophes, either individually or communally, without looking at the way the media covers such events and how it influences what we think. It has an enormous impact on our sense of personal security and our collective ability to recover.

I have an acute understanding of how journalists behave from inside the industry, but I have no idea how it feels to be the person at the other end of a story, when everybody in the community wants to know what happened to you, and journalists are fighting to land your exclusive interview. What might somebody who's experienced that teach us about the aftermath of a blindside? And what if we had the empathy to imagine that one day we might be that person?

I remember somebody the media once dubbed 'The Ice Man', and I send him an email, asking to meet.

'James Scott . . . James Scott . . .' Friends would search their brains when I mentioned I was flying to Brisbane to interview him for this book.

'You know, he was the medical student who survived forty-three days lost in the Himalayas,' I'd prompt.

Blank faces.

'It was a huge story twenty years ago, one of the greatest survival stories of all time,' I'd urge.

'Um, rings a vague bell,' they'd say.

'The guy with the Mars Bar!' I'd finally blurt.

'Oh, I remember him!'

This was the response nearly every time.

The 1992 rescue of Brisbane medical student James Scott after he became lost in Nepal was one of the biggest stories of my career. His survival was so extraordinary that an American medical journal concluded that elements of it were beyond scientific explanation. Yet the only detail most Australians remember is that he reportedly had a Mars Bar in his backpack.

Here's the scoop: it wasn't a Mars Bar. The most famous detail of James Scott's story is a myth. But more about that later.

Today, James is Associate Professor Scott, a highly respected psychiatrist specialising in child and adolescent mental health at the University of Queensland and the Royal Brisbane Hospital. Almost twenty-five years after his ordeal in the Himalayas, he still hears a Mars Bar gag at least once a fortnight.

'This week, I went and saw the movie *Sully*, I don't know if you've seen it yet,' James says when we meet in his office near the hospital. He has short reddish hair, a boyish smile and an intelligent, inquisitive face.

'No, but I'm keen to,' I say.

In the film, Tom Hanks plays US Airways pilot Chesley 'Sully' Sullenberger, who in 2009 landed a jumbo jet on the Hudson River after it flew into a flock of geese and lost both engines. Incredibly, all 155 people on board survived.

'Go see it, it's a good movie. The part that really resonated with me is one moment when he's at a bar. Everyone is friendly, "Oh it's great to see you," and stuff,' says James. 'Then they go, "We've named a drink after you. We've called it The Sully – it's Wild Goose with a splash of water." It was referencing the geese and they all thought it was hilarious. Sully didn't. I thought, That's kind of like every time someone makes a joke about a Mars Bar.'

The reason the Mars Bar is so memorable is that, improbably, it became the central detail in a phenomenal media frenzy surrounding James Scott's miraculous survival. His experience, from the point of his rescue onwards, illustrates how stressful and damaging intense media interest can be for ordinary people who inadvertently find themselves in the middle of something extraordinary. When the public becomes fascinated by these kinds of stories and journalists descend, a heavy toll can be exacted on the person in the centre.

In 1991, James Scott was twenty-two years old and a final-year medical student when he signed up for a four-week practical elective at the Bir Hospital in Kathmandu, planning to combine the internship with some recreational hiking. On 22 December, he headed off on a trek and made a decision that turned out to be extremely unfortunate. He was crossing a high-altitude pass with a companion when clouds moved in and snow fell. James decided to turn back while the other man continued over the pass. As the weather deteriorated, James was unable to find the tea house he had slept in the previous night and became lost. He initially tried to find his way out, but the snow was too deep and the cliffs too treacherous.

James had intended to take advantage of the food, water and accommodation in tea houses along the track on which he'd started, and so he had insufficient supplies for the conditions in which he found himself. After he was eventually rescued, close to death, it was his shame and guilt at his own carelessness that caused him the most pain, not his physical injuries.

During the forty-three days that he was lost, James was taken to his limits physically, mentally and emotionally. He began the ordeal as a very fit and secure young man but was quickly starving, dehydrated and freezing, and there was nothing he could do but wait for what seemed certain to be an extremely painful and lonely death.

The famous chocolate in his backpack was plain Cadbury Dairy Milk, not a Mars Bar. He ate it early in his ordeal and it had no bearing on his survival. In his book about his misadventure, *Lost in the Himalayas*, James writes in great detail of his suffering, recalling that he would occasionally tear at his hair or pinch his skin to remind himself that the pain he felt could be worse. The first night was such misery, it is hard to conceive that he endured weeks afterwards: 'My hands were blue and my teeth chattered incessantly and this would be the first of many nights that I would feel the cold more than I could ever have imagined. It was not the superficial cold that most people can relate to, but a deep chilling cold that feels as if it's killing the very life within. The cold was like pain. Just as it seemed as bad as it could possibly get, it got worse and the suffering increased. I was sure it would be impossible to be as cold as I was and still survive the night.'

James was furious at himself and also devastated by the anguish he knew his disappearance would be causing at home. He feared his body would never be found, exacerbating his family's grief.

The amount of time James survived on the mountain was undoubtedly miraculous, but there are explanations for some aspects of it. His medical studies furnished him with vital knowledge – for example, he didn't eat snow without first melting it and he paced his intake so as to not reduce his core body temperature. He knew he would lose most of his body heat through his head so he wrapped it in towels and clothes. He was helped too by his personal qualities, especially his physical fitness but also his mental resilience. He occupied himself in ways that kept his hope of rescue alive. James had close relationships with his family, friends and fiancée, and until his pen ran out of ink he wrote to tell them how much he loved them. He replayed in his mind happy experiences from his life in as much detail as he could. He sniffed a stick of Old Spice deodorant when his spirits were low as it reminded him of home. As a Christian, he prayed for hours. And he credits in particular the discipline of karate (in which he had a black belt) with helping save his life. James spent hours mentally performing *kata*, sequences of techniques that flow one into the other. These are detailed and intricate and James could calmly occupy himself for long stretches of time, meticulously recreating them in his mind.

Yet even with that formidable arsenal of coping tools, by his final days on the mountain, James was suicidal and weighing up various options. Ultimately, as for Walter Mikac, it was thoughts of his family that stopped him.

On 2 February 1992, the Scott family paid for one final rescue helicopter to do a sweep across the mountains. So much time had elapsed that almost everybody thought it was futile, or that at best the mission would recover a body. Incredibly, the helicopter spotted the emaciated James. But instead of being the end of his ordeal, it marked the beginning of a different one.

By the day of the rescue, the media had long moved on to more fruitful stories, giving up James Scott for dead. When he was found alive, it prompted one of the most intense media frenzies of my years in journalism. A live broadcast of the cricket was interrupted with the news that the young student had been found alive. The race to land the first interview with James began, and that was when media from all over the world dubbed him 'The Ice Man'. Reporters besieged his family. James was being treated at the Patan Hospital in Lalitpur, the city next to Kathmandu, and it was very quickly overrun. A Third World facility, it struggled to function at the best of times and now it crawled with journalists and photographers. Attempts were made to steal James's medical records and photographers tried to climb through a window into his room. One reporter pretended to be from a travel insurance company to talk his way inside, unsuccessfully.

This chaos unfolded as James lay close to death. His temperature was so low that it didn't even register on a thermometer, and severe malnutrition had taken him close to organ failure and also damaged his vision, causing scenes in front of his eyes to shake violently and making it hard for him to recognise faces. He was highly unstable emotionally, vacillating from euphoria at being alive to weeping in despair and begging to be put back under the rock on the mountain.

James's sister Joanne went to Nepal to be with him and she tried to shield him as much as possible. It was only when he was medically transferred from Nepal to the Royal Brisbane Hospital that he realised something strange was happening.

'When we flew into Singapore, I remember there was a lot of banging on the ambulance, and photographs. Then we came to Brisbane; there it was again. I had a very good friend come to visit and I said, "What's news?" and he said, "You are,"' James recalls.

'Was the level of interest problematic for you in terms of your recovery?' I ask.

'I think enormously. When any of us get hurt or traumatised, all you want is to be with people you can trust. And the media and the whole general, public interest meant I had to be talking to a whole lot of people I didn't know. It was kind of not what was best for me at the time.'

'Did you or anyone in your family know anyone in the media, or did you have any experience with journalists?'

When James shakes his head I ask, 'So how did you figure out what to do?'

'The family was just getting bombarded with phone calls. They tried to address it but the more interviews they did, the more requests they got. Dad then went and appealed to the media and said, "Can you back off a bit?" He got broadly criticised – "How dare you tell us to try and do that." My father was with the University of Queensland at the time, so he went to the media relations people and said, "Can you please help us?" I think at this stage, offers were flying in: if I did this interview or that one, I'd get X amount of dollars.'

Money was definitely an issue for James. His family had spent tens of thousands of dollars on the rescue effort in Nepal. James was also extremely anxious about whether he would be able to return to medical school, or indeed make any sort of living in the future, given that his vision was now so compromised. He had no idea how his health would pan out in the long term.

Desperate for help, and on the recommendation of his university colleagues, James's father rang an agent named Harry M. Miller. Miller was then the biggest name in celebrity management in Australia. He also handled people who had become accidentally famous and landed in the centre of gigantic media bidding wars, such as Lindy Chamberlain. Once Miller stepped in, the relief for the Scott family was immediate. The media harassment stopped overnight because now everything went through Miller's office. Very quickly, the agent tied up a deal with the Nine Network's *60 Minutes* for an exclusive, paid interview with James.

The Scott family's relief quickly turned to alarm and concern as they watched what happened next. In the media, James's story started to morph into something they didn't recognise, shifting away from his miraculous survival to a more sceptical bent: how could such a fantastic story be true? Did The Ice Man fake his ordeal? Was he a charlatan looking for a way to make a buck?

Three factors arguably drove this new angle. First, the public was still obsessed by the story but there was an information vacuum, because James was not yet well enough to talk. Journalists were therefore desperately casting around for ways to keep the story going. Second, Channel Nine's competitors were annoyed that it had stitched up an exclusive and so they started looking for ways to lessen the appeal of the 'product' Nine had bought – that is to say, James Scott. In the business, this is known as a 'spoiler'. (*Frontline*, the brilliant satire of TV current affairs shows, parodied the Scott story not long after the real-life events: when the team misses out on an interview with a woman dubbed 'The Desert Angel', who survived weeks lost in the desert, they promote a spoiler with the tagline, 'Desert Angel – or Desert Devil?') The third factor was a major hoax that had occurred just weeks before James's rescue, when a Gold Coast woman named Fairlie Arrow staged her own abduction. This had been a huge story in Australia, and it meant that the possibility of a scam was buzzing loudly in the hive mind.

In the midst of all this, the chocolate bar started to become a problem. The early reporting of James's survival mentioned that the only food he'd had was a chocolate bar, and the public was dying to know what sort. Rumours took hold that it was a Mars Bar. It was one of those irrelevant but colourful details with which everybody became irrationally obsessed.

'I think this is where Harry didn't give good advice,' James says. 'I think Harry was counting the dollars and thinking, We can probably get a contract with a chocolate bar company, and all this stuff. I think Harry had gone to every chocolate bar company saying, "We can get James Scott to endorse your product." Harry was pushing a lot. His instructions to me were, "For fuck's sake, don't tell anyone about the chocolate bar, whatever you fucking do."'

When James eventually recorded his *60 Minutes* interview, it ended up delivering one of the most famous and tense exchanges in the program's history. The reporter Richard Carleton, known for his take-no-prisoners approach, began to grill James about what kind of chocolate bar it was.

'I was really stuck in the middle of Harry ordering me, "Don't say what brand of chocolate bar," and Richard asking, "What is the brand of the chocolate bar?" That got him [Richard] really inflamed: "Is this guy really for real?"'

'In hindsight, do you think you were well enough to do that interview?' I ask.

'No. Not at all,' James says. 'I think Richard Carleton was the wrong person to do it as well. I don't think that's how you treat someone who's been very traumatised. Once you start with that really interrogative interview style, I think anyone who's been traumatised goes into fight-or-flight mode. I completely lost it, I was distressed that what should have been such a positive story ended up in such a difficult altercation. It was hard for me to understand how it happened. We didn't go into the interview with ill will. I was just trying to tell my story. I can see it from Richard's perspective too. We didn't handle it well from our end either.'

The reluctance to simply name the chocolate bar gave the whole thing way more significance than it ever deserved and somehow, the false information that it was a Mars Bar took firm root in the mind of the public.

'Would you do things differently if you had the time again?' I ask.

'I think I'd still engage somebody to manage it. You just cannot manage it. That was the right way to go. I think identifying the right journalist to tell the story is important. I think there are journalists who can do that sort of inquisitive approach, being empathetically curious about what happened,' he says.

James doesn't regret selling the story either, even though it caused him so much grief.

'If there's money to be made, you may as well make it, because you're going to cop it either way. That's kind of driven my views,' James says.

'To be honest, that's my view too, even though I work for the ABC,' I tell him. 'Other people are making money from it.'

'Of course they are. It's a capitalist society. You've got a product, that product's got value,' James says.

'Some of these lessons you only know because you went through it.'

'Yeah. You're really at your most vulnerable if you're not media-savvy and such.'

James eventually made a full emotional recovery from his trauma, but nearly twenty-five years later he still carries physical scars. He has permanent double vision and balance problems, meaning he had to give up the karate that helped keep him alive on the mountain. His injuries also prevented him from pursuing the career he had hoped to have in surgery, although he is content in psychiatry.

'Not many people in their lives are ever tested like you were, on every level simultaneously,' I say. 'Emotionally, mentally, physically, every way you could imagine. How about the challenges in your life since then? Has the fact that you survived that situation given you confidence to cope with other challenges?'

'I think it probably has but I don't consciously relate it back. Like, I was seeing a group of friends the other day and we were talking about something and one of my very good friends said, "It's like James, he's unflappable." I never think of myself that way. But maybe having been through that, I don't get so excited about things. I don't think, This has happened, but it's not as bad as Nepal; it's not that sort of conscious link.'

'Do you feel there was a lasting psychological legacy from it?' I ask.

'I think my Christian faith is the lasting legacy from it. I suppose the nature of having faith, you have a lot of doubts, especially being a scientist. But then I kind of go back and think, It's just an extra-ordinary thing to happen. That's my explanation for it,' James says.

Like Louisa, James might have faith but he doesn't hold any 'ratbag delusion' that God has singled him out. When I ask him whether he thinks it was God's plan for him to survive that experience for some higher purpose, he laughs.

'No,' he says.

'Was it just luck?'

'I can't explain it,' James replies, looking almost apologetic for not offering me some profound wisdom about the mysteries of fate.

Once James Scott found himself in the middle of such an incredible survival tale, it was always going to turn into a media circus. It's unsettling to hear how troubling it was to him because here's the thing: I would have conducted that *60 Minutes* interview much the same way. I definitely would have been one of those reporters badgering the Scott family after the rescue and if I hadn't been able to get an interview with them, I almost certainly would have chased the angle of whether the survival tale was credible. There's no doubt I would have asked about the chocolate bar.

I've always thought I'm a decent human being but what does it say about me and about the practice of journalism that even with everything James has told me, my instinct is that what happened to him was not only understandable, it was mostly justifiable? I have intellectually understood for a long time that journalists have a duty to think more deeply about these questions because we owe something to the people on whom we report. We are using survivors and victims to help the community understand its thoughts and feelings about how the world works, and so, at the very least, we should do as little harm as possible in pursuit of the story.

Meeting James makes me think about these things in a less abstract way. Where is the balance between the cost to the individual and the public's desire to know the story? As James points out, it's the media that profits the most from high-profile stories, not the person at the centre of them. The Nine Network would have made far more in advertising dollars from The Ice Man exclusive than it paid James. That's why everybody was in a bidding war in the first place – it was a story the public wanted to hear, and that translates into eyeballs on the product, and in turn profit.

There is of course a question about whether there was a legitimate public interest in James Scott's story or whether it was simply that the public was curious. These are two different things. Take the case of one of Louisa Hope's fellow Lindt Café survivors, Julie Taylor. She has never told her story in the media. Julie was pregnant during the siege, which must have added a huge layer of complexity to the terror. She fled the café not long before the siege ended in the death of her best friend, Katrina Dawson. I would be very interested to hear her story, but do I believe it's in the public interest for Julie Taylor to tell it? I do not. There has already been an extensive examination of the events of that day, and the coronial inquiry turned over every last shred of evidence. Julie Taylor was a witness in those hearings. It is a sound assumption that there's nothing she can share further that will change what we already know, or that would have fresh implications for the law, policing or public safety. There is no valid public interest argument for her story, regardless of how intriguing it may be.

I also accept that there was no real public interest implication in what happened to James Scott. There aren't hundreds of Australians getting constantly lost on snowy mountains. Nonetheless, it was one of the most miraculous survival feats in recorded history, something that spoke to our human drive to live. It was worth having on the record for that reason alone, and nobody could tell that story except James himself. Unlike the Lindt Café, there weren't seventeen other people there. The public was desperate to hear details and I would have felt as a journalist that it was my job to try to deliver them.

Journalism has a culture that values and rewards breaking news, fresh angles that keep stories on the front page and juicy details that make people talk. From day one in journalism school, you're taught that while you must behave ethically towards the people on whom you report, ultimately you serve the public above all else. That means I would justify most of the media behaviour towards James Scott and his family – excluding diabolical things like lying to get into his hospital room – on the grounds that it was a story for which the public had an insatiable hunger. Rightly or wrongly, the cost to James would have been a secondary consideration, particularly once he agreed to take money in exchange for telling the story.

The decisions journalists make are driven not only by the industry's culture or by competitive pressure; there are also personal considerations that come into play, as for any human being doing a job. I can't tell you how many times I've been on a plane, assigned to cover some big event, with a sick feeling in the pit of my stomach: what if I can't find something to file? What if another reporter gets something massive that I don't? I've never failed to file a story in twenty-five years but I certainly know the humiliation of being scooped. Breaking stories is the core task of a journalist, and missing something that somebody else reports is failure. As bad as it feels to approach people like the Scotts when they've been through such an ordeal, it feels worse to not make that phone call and then watch a competitor interview them on another network while your boss stands alongside you, silently watching too. Like any employee, you fear for your job security, your reputation and your future prospects.

In a case like James Scott's, there is an unfortunate collision between two forces. Maximum public curiosity and therefore maximum media harassment coincide with the peak vulnerability of the people involved. Not surprisingly, the early weeks after a traumatic event are usually when people are least able to talk to the media and also least able to judge whether they should. In February 2009, one of the most devastating bushfires in Australian history tore through Victoria, killing 173 people on a day that became known as Black Saturday. Months afterwards, a university study found that many of the traumatised survivors who had spoken to journalists could not even recall being interviewed.

That study, carried out by the Centre for Advanced Journalism at Melbourne University, spoke to twenty-eight journalists who had covered the Black Saturday fires and to twenty-seven survivors they had interviewed. The researchers noted that the pressures on journalists were acute and that it wasn't surprising that 'errors of judgment are made, inconsistencies abound, blind eyes are turned, ethical lapses occur, compromises are made, and . . . the interests of the affected public fade into the background'. They noted that there was little evidence of journalists acting in bad faith, yet good intentions themselves were not enough to guard against lapses. Even so, the research found that most of those twenty-seven survivors felt their experience with journalists was generally positive and that the media did a good job.

There's one important difference to note between an event like Black Saturday and a story like James Scott's: on Black Saturday, the victims vastly outnumbered the media. In James's case, it was dozens of journalists all homing in on one person.

Maybe you buy some of the pressures that journalists face as an excuse for the way we sometimes behave and maybe you don't. Even if you believe most of what I've said about the validity of chasing James Scott's story, how about my other outrageous claim: that I would have interviewed James in much the same way as Richard Carleton did, even though James has explicitly told me how hurtful it was? First, there's a stigma about paying people for their stories (chequebook journalism), and I would have been keen to prove that I wasn't going soft on James just because my network had paid him. By the time of James's interview, there were questions about the credibility of his survival tale, most unjustly, but they could not be ignored. I would have considered I was giving him a chance to correct the public record by asking about this.

Second, even though the chocolate was a silly side issue, a journalist is there to ask what the public wants to know, and the public wanted to know the brand of chocolate. I accept that this is not as sound a reason as my first, but as I pointed out earlier, I've been schooled to believe that if the public wants to know something, I should ask about it.

Third, once James declined to reveal that information, I would have doubled down, just as Carleton did, confused about why James wasn't forthcoming. I would have considered it a dent in his credibility, and been annoyed that while Nine had paid for the full story, James was withholding not just information, but one of the key details viewers wanted to know more about. The chocolate bar had become tantalising because it was being kept so hush-hush – *why* was it so important? If James had answered Richard Carleton's question with, 'It was just plain Cadbury chocolate,' everybody would have moved on and *60 Minutes* probably would have focused mostly on what James wanted – the miracle of surviving against such overwhelming odds.

Would I have worried about subjecting James to a fairly rigorous interview when his health was fragile? Yes, but I still would have been tough, justifying it on the grounds that it was his decision to strike the deal and do the interview, and the risk was therefore his. That is defensible thinking for a journalist. Is it defensible thinking for an empathetic human being?

When I look back at the mistakes I've made as a reporter, including experiences that to this day make me feel ashamed, I can see that they were usually due to a failure of empathy. I've never made a deliberate effort to lie, mislead or skew. I've never actively set out to hurt somebody. Sometimes I have made errors of fact due to carelessness, ignorance, haste or misspeaking (the last being something that is hard to avoid 100 per cent of the time on live television). The mistakes that niggle me most, though, relate to questionable decisions I've made in the process of gathering material for broadcast, due to the pressure of deadlines, my ambition to deliver a cracking story, or my own lack of maturity and compassion.

In 1994, when I was twenty-one, I worked for the Nine Network in Brisbane on a local news/lifestyle hybrid called *Extra*, which led into the 6 pm news. I was desperately eager to make a good impression and move up the newsroom ladder. As the most junior person in the place, I did all manner of jobs, including rolling the autocue, printing scripts, answering the phone, preparing research briefs for journalists, and assigning camera crews. Eventually I was allowed to have a stab at reporting a few stories myself.

One story I pitched was about children who have difficulty making friends – why does it happen and what can parents do? We arranged to film some footage at a primary school near the TV station, and I briefed the cameraman to keep an eye out in the playground for any children who were sitting alone. I asked him to make sure they weren't identifiable but to shoot in such a way that it was clear they were isolated. There is always one such child in any schoolyard and when the cameraman returned with the footage, he had filmed a little girl left out of the play. She was shot from a distance and a hat shielded her face, although her long, platinum-blond hair poked out from under it.

I interviewed a school principal and a psychologist and the story came together fine. It went to air and my boss liked it. As I was preparing to head home, merry with self-satisfaction, the main office phone rang and I answered it. It was the father of the blond girl. He told me that I had publicly identified his daughter as a child with no friends.

No I didn't, I told him, I'd deliberately asked the cameraman to make sure the child could not be identified. Of course she couldn't be identified by a stranger, he replied, but look at her hair! Every child, every teacher, every parent at that school could recognise his daughter, he said. And not only that, he went on, they were all so excited to be on television that every last one of them would have watched the story. He finished by telling me that his daughter did have a lot of trouble making friends and that I had made the situation worse by labelling her that way in front of all her classmates.

I was gutted, of course, and now, more than twenty years later, I'm still appalled that I didn't see the obvious point he was making before I put the story to air. I had next to no experience, so I'll offer that in my defence, but really? I didn't have the basic common sense to see that the child would be recognisable to every last person in her circle, and that it might be a problem? I can truthfully say that I didn't think of that, but I do wonder if on some level I chose to ignore any qualms because I needed pictures to tell the story on television. The whole episode still upsets me and I am ashamed to share it publicly.

About a year after that, I was working for the ABC when the newsroom chief of staff sent me on a light plane to Windera, some 200 kilometres north-west of Brisbane, where I went on a raid of a cattle farm with the Police Stock Squad and the RSPCA. A farmer was in trouble for allowing his cows to starve. I recall feeling disgusted as we walked around the property in blistering heat. The animals were skeletal and there were several carcasses lying in a dusty, parched paddock, looking like deflated balloons. The farmer arrived home partway through the raid. He had a number of children with him but I can't recall seeing his wife. I remember looking at him with contempt and wondering what sort of awful person would let their animals suffer like this.

I recently rewatched this story for the first time in twenty-one years and noticed that I'd reported it as a straight animal cruelty story. I had not interviewed the farmer; I can't recall now if that was because he refused or because I didn't ask. The thing that strikes me today is that even though I mentioned drought in the story, at no point did I explore the question of why the animals were starving. I couldn't get past my own shock at their condition. Were they starving because the farmer's family was also starving? I did report that there was feed in the shed on the property and yet I didn't ask why, since feed was available, the animals had not been fed. It was a pathetic piece of reporting on my part because I lacked the empathy to put myself in the farmer's shoes, and so I came nowhere near telling the real story and nor did I do the right thing by him.

I'd like to put both those episodes down to youthful inexperience, but sadly, I can identify similar mistakes when I was a senior reporter. In 2005, more than a decade later, I was the ABC's US correspondent, based in Washington DC. I was sent to New Orleans when an epic hurricane hit America's southern coastline. Hurricane Katrina basically wiped New Orleans off the map. On my second or third day there, I made it to the city's airport terminal, by that time the scene of the evacuation of tens of thousands of residents. Many of them had been at the city's convention centre for several days prior to the evacuation, with no food or running water and no way to communicate with their families. They were angry, traumatised, and in some cases hostile.

I was at the airport looking for a story for ABC Radio's *AM* program. I had a couple of hours to find something to report and transmit to Australia. One of the people I interviewed was an elderly African American woman who was in tears and probably shock. She didn't know where several of her family members were and she listed them by name. She had four or five grandchildren with her, the eldest of whom looked about ten.

I knew I had struck journalistic gold. She was emotional and she had a compelling story to tell. I asked question after question to prompt her to keep talking. The longer we went on, the more emotional she became. I was thinking, Just one more question, I just have to keep her going a little bit longer to have enough for a story. Finally, in a soft voice, the ten-year-old said, 'That's enough.' I pretended not to hear him and asked another question. 'That's enough,' he said more boldly. I then wrapped it up. To this day, it mortifies me that it took a ten-year-old boy to tell me when enough was enough. Twice.

The thing is, if you asked me where I would rank myself on a scale of journalists, where 1 is a psychopath and 10 is a decent person trying to do the right thing, I'd give myself a 10. I would say you'd be lucky if I were the journalist to knock on your door. Yet I've just laid bare some examples that suggest I can be as mercenary and reptilian as anyone. There may be some journalists who have never made the mistakes I have, but I suspect that, if we're honest, many of us would have to admit to acting less than ideally under pressure.

I don't often talk to my colleagues about these issues. We don't sit around discussing what goes into making the sausage. I know very little about how other journalists persuade people to do interviews, or how they deal with survivors they meet in disaster zones or in the aftermath of great trauma. An American psychologist and academic, Dr Elana Newman, has noted an historical avoidance of scholarship regarding trauma and journalism. She suggests that this may be because journalists don't want to think about the connection as it forces them to confront the fact that they often benefit from others' misery.

That Hurricane Katrina story that caused a ten-year-old to pull me up for harassing his grandma? Nominated for Australia's highest journalism honour, a Walkley Award. In Dr Newman's words: 'While journalists do not create the conditions they cover, many recognise that they do receive awards and recognition for telling the public about these calamities and repugnant situations. Thus, the relative lack of scholarly investigation of trauma in the news may be continuously shaped by a tension inherent in acknowledging and avoiding the impact of trauma more broadly.'

It's an uncomfortable thought: we journalists may not like thinking about these questions because it might force us to change the way we operate. Despite the aversion, though, what would happen if more journalists did front up to these questions? What might we learn?

On the morning of 10 January 2011, Amanda Gearing could not believe the intensity of the downpour she was watching through the window of her study in Toowoomba. It was as if some sort of artillery in the sky were bombarding the earth with water. Bullets of rain ricocheted off the driveway and within minutes a violent brown torrent was invading the street. The ferocity of the onslaught itself was strange enough, but Amanda's house was perched on one of Toowoomba's highest points, the last place you'd ever expect to see a flood. In fourteen years of living there, Amanda had never seen anything remotely like it.

What she didn't know at the time was that she was witnessing a superstorm, created by the collision of two intense thunderstorms off the coast of south-east Queensland earlier that morning. The rivers and dams of Toowoomba and its surrounds were already full and the soil sodden, thanks to a record wet season, and when this superstorm hit, it caused what police would later call 'an instant inland tsunami'.

In the foothills of the Great Dividing Range and on the coastal plain east of the city, the water moved so fast and with such force that hundreds of residents were caught unawares in their homes, cars and shops. One minute people were pottering about in their kitchens, the next they were running for their lives. Many of those attempting to drive to safety in their cars and trucks were swept off roads by a wall of water crashing on them without warning. In numerous cases, bystanders – themselves lucky to escape death – watched aghast and powerless as the flood swept away friends and neighbours.

By the time the rain stopped and the water subsided, thirty-three men, women and children were dead, with three more missing, presumed dead. Nineteen of those deaths were in the Lockyer Valley, a picturesque area of rolling fruit and vegetable farmlands some 20 kilometres from Toowoomba (and about an hour's drive west of Brisbane). One of the valley's towns, Grantham, lost twelve people in just two hours from a population of about five hundred, a tragedy that made global news and prompted a visit by Prince William.

As Amanda Gearing watched from her window on the morning of the storm, she had no idea of the extent of the catastrophe. She would find out soon enough. Amanda was a journalist, meant to be taking a step back from daily news reporting to work on academic research, but early that afternoon she had a call from the Brisbane chief of staff for *The Australian* newspaper, who'd been hearing reports of massive flooding, widespread destruction and an overwhelmed emergency services network. Could Amanda file some freelance stories for them? She grabbed her notebook and mobile phone, organised a photographer and ventured out.

Amanda was no young cowboy reporter trying to make a name on a big story. She was a very experienced, competent journalist with years of reporting in outback Queensland behind her, covering every kind of story imaginable. She was fifty years old and a mother of four. When you operate as a solo reporter in a regional area of Australia, invariably accidents, tragedies and deaths become a staple. You can't hide in a big newsroom, ducking and weaving every time the chief of staff is hunting for somebody to go and solicit a photograph from a family whose sixteen-year-old has been killed. You're the only person available for 'death knock' duty. In Amanda's years of working in Toowoomba, she had become particularly experienced at death knocks, performing dozens for Brisbane's *Courier-Mail*.

Like most journalists, I am terrified of doing death knocks and will do anything to avoid them, so I'm fascinated by Amanda's experience. I contact her via Skype and I ask her whether she has any particular technique to encourage people to talk.

Amanda says, 'It was that I didn't ask them to. Because I put myself in their position, the only thing I could do was think, If this was me, what would I do? And it did not feel right for me to go to someone's house who had just lost their husband or their wife, or run over their child, or whatever they had done, and say, "Can you give me information, can you give me a story, can you give me anything?" I couldn't ask for a glass of water. But what I could do was say, "The process you're entering is a difficult process. It will go on for a couple of years." And I did feel that I could give them empathy, be sorry for the loss, which I was. I could give them information about the process they were entering. I could give them information about what the police were already saying and ask them, "Is there anything you would like to say?" I would say, "There is going to be a story in the paper about this. If there is anything you would like to say about your child or husband or wife, the paper is interested now. Next week, they probably won't be so interested." More often than not, they did. Ninety per cent of them did.'

That regular exposure to death meant that by the time Amanda ventured out into the floods in January 2011, she was extremely experienced at speaking to people in the midst of the unimaginable. Even so, the scale of the loss and trauma she came across in the Lockyer Valley was beyond anything she had ever seen.

There was Daniel McGuire, a member of the Grantham Rural Fire Service. When the Lockyer Creek broke its banks, he attempted to evacuate his 31-year-old wife, Llync, and their three children, Jocelyn, five, Garry, twelve, and Zachary, seven, in a rural fire truck. But a violent wave of water, taller than the truck, crashed down on them as they were driving out of their yard. Daniel saved Zachary by pushing him out of the car window and onto a tree. The force of the water then propelled Daniel out of the cabin and he managed to clamber up a tree too. But the family members remaining in the truck couldn't escape and all three drowned as it sank.

Daniel and Zach clung to their branches for six hours, until the water receded enough for them to climb down to safety. Daniel told Amanda that if he'd not been able to hear Zach's voice, he would have let himself slide into the water too, with the rest of the family.

Amanda also met Peter and Marie Van Straten, a retired couple who had watched from inside their highset Queenslander as roiling water flooded the main street of Grantham. Within seconds, geysers began spurting through the floorboards of their shaking house. A tree smashed through the bedroom wall and suddenly the house was dislodged from its moorings and began to float away. It crashed into a tree and the kitchen was ripped off. Peter and Marie struggled through the rapidly rising water, trying to get to the centre of the house as rooms crumbled around them. Two kilometres down the road, the house came to rest in a paddock, lodged against something. Now that it was no longer moving, it started filling up with water even faster.

Marie had a broken arm and Peter had no medication for his diabetes. Soon the water was up to Peter's neck and over Marie's head. He stood on one leg, pulling the other one up for Marie to sit on to get her head above the surface. As it grew dark, they began to lose hope. Peter was grey and hypothermic; Marie started to sob. Miraculously, after they'd said their goodbyes to each other, a helicopter flew over the area and they attracted its attention and were rescued.

Along with Amanda's reporting for *The Australian*, she produced a Walkley Award-winning radio documentary called *The Day That Changed Grantham* and wrote a book called *The Torrent*, which went into even more detail. In the process of her investigation, she was niggled by a broader question not directly related to the flood or its causes: what makes people decide to talk to journalists at times of immense trauma? The thought was prompted by one particular survivor's initial refusal to grant an interview.

'He lost his mother, his mother-in-law and his baby daughter, and he almost lost his wife, his two other children, and he almost died, and he lost his house,' Amanda tells me. 'I thought, It's not surprising that he's not talking to me but what about these others? They are. Why are they doing this? If I was in that state, I'd be flat out getting breakfast or getting out of bed. But they're fronting up for interviews and are willing to talk.'

Amanda was stunned to discover that there was very little research into why traumatised people speak to reporters and what that might teach us about the practice of journalism. In recent years, it has been acknowledged that journalists who cover traumatic events are susceptible to the same professional hazards, including post-traumatic stress disorder, as other first responders.

There is a growing body of research and training for journalists on how to protect themselves from this, largely led by Columbia University's excellent Dart Center for Journalism & Trauma. But at the victims' end of the equation, Amanda realised, there was a gap in the research. She was still writing a proposal for a thesis and figured this was a solid topic for exploration. Alongside her investigation into the flood's causes and its aftermath, she added one simple question for survivors: Why did you decide to speak to a reporter?

Any experienced journalist would be able to give an anecdotal answer to that question. The University of Melbourne's report on Black Saturday, discussed earlier, touches on it, although it mostly focuses on the experience of being interviewed by a journalist and satisfaction or otherwise with the published work, not the reasons for talking in the first place. Amanda's study – from her admittedly small sample of thirty-three – is unique, and interesting because it actually qualifies some of those reasons, identifying six main ones.

The most common was the hope that it might aid personal recovery. That was closely followed by the desire for the public to truly understand what had happened. Many of the victims felt that while media coverage of the disaster had been extensive, it had not captured just how devastating it was and how long-term the impact would be. The next two reasons were closely related: people wanted lessons to be learned from the tragedy, and they felt a sense of duty to ensure that responses to future disasters were improved. The fifth reason, perhaps an obvious one, was timing: the decision to talk was influenced by when the request for an interview was made and whether, at that moment, the person felt up to sharing their story. The final reason was possibly the most surprising, yet it was mentioned by more than one person – it was good to talk to somebody who would listen for free.

Daniel McGuire, the man whose wife and two children died in the rural fire truck, told Amanda, 'It's better talking to you than to a psychologist because I can talk to someone without paying them to listen to me.' Another Lockyer Valley resident, Rod Alford, told her, 'I find it more relaxing talking to you than the highly educated professionals. They tend to be more financially focused – they are watching their clock and say, "Time's up – would you like to make another appointment?" And I think, You bastards – you're caring and sharing for two hours, but only because you're being paid.'

Of course, journalists are also paid to listen, just not by the victims. And journalists can sometimes profit from hearing the stories of survivors in a way that psychologists don't. Amanda was talking and listening to the flood victims first and foremost to get a story, one for which she earned income and was given an award by her peers. She had something to gain from the interviews, but obviously she was also caring enough in the way she handled them for the interviewees to feel that they too had benefited.

Both the flood and bushfire studies asked survivors if anything about dealing with journalists had made their situation worse. People reported that they'd sometimes felt used when journalists appeared on the scene soon after the disaster, conducted an interview, left and were never heard from again. It was also hurtful if the journalist seemed rushed or eager to leave as soon as they had the pictures or story they were after. Survivors were upset if images of them appearing extremely distressed were published when permission hadn't been sought, particularly if the footage was used repeatedly. The bushfire survivors were incensed if they intuited that a journalist was trying to ask questions to force an emotional response and make them cry. For the flood victims, it was very distressing when a report included inaccuracies, no matter how tiny.

'The family of that person will cut that paper out and keep it forever. It will have my name at the top,' Amanda says. 'And if I've misspelled the name, if I have the day wrong, or the time wrong, or the colour of the car wrong – some, in a sense, inconsequential thing to the death – it doesn't matter. It's a big error in their eyes. And I don't want anyone who keeps something like that, that is so important to them, to think, Yeah, well, they did die and that stupid journalist couldn't even get the time right or the colour of the car right. It's about care. Did she care?'

The Black Saturday researchers asked survivors to imagine they were sitting around with a few young journalists who had no experience in covering disasters. What advice would they give about how to treat victims? Their answers could be summed up in four words: humanity (don't lose sight of the fact that you're dealing with people, not characters in a story), empathy (try to understand what the person is going through and act accordingly), autonomy (allow the subject to lead the discussion), and respect (make allowances, give the person time and space, and above all, don't be exploitative).

In Amanda's thesis, she formulated guidelines too: be flexible with interview timing and location; empower interviewees to understand that they don't have to answer every question they are asked; be scrupulously committed to accuracy; and give the interviewee emotional security – for example, by not interrupting them to ask questions.

'When I did the first few stories, as I listened back to the recordings to transcribe them, I heard them talk and then I heard myself butt in with a question,' she recalls. 'I realised that the person I was talking to never came back to that point. They could never find that original thread that they were on. I missed all the rest of the story or I missed a substantial chunk of what was going on for them. I kicked myself. "You fool. Shut up. Just shut up and listen."' Clearly, that is the type of interview James Scott wishes he'd had with *60 Minutes*.

Through her research, Amanda also realised that if journalists could listen effectively, they might help lay the groundwork for future counsellors – or at least do no harm. For more experienced journalists, this kind of approach can be second nature, but for junior reporters or for journalists under deadline or competitive pressure, it can slip by the wayside, as my own Hurricane Katrina experience amply illustrates.

Amanda leaves me with a thought-provoking idea.

'For every journalist who does a death knock,' she says, 'I think it should be routine that they go back a week or fortnight or so later, and ask the question, "Why did you agree to talk to me?"

I think we need vastly more data than thirty-three answers to that question. Journalists all over the world today will be at scenes of death and disasters and they will be asking the public to talk to them. And none of them will go back and ever ask why.'

After I wrote this chapter, I emailed it to James Scott. I didn't want him to be taken by surprise on publication of this book, when he read that I would have conducted his *60 Minutes* interview almost identically to Richard Carleton, even though James had found it so traumatic.

'Does that make me a bad person?' I asked.

'No, it doesn't make you a bad person. You're adhering to the principles that are fundamental to your profession,' James wrote back, quite generously I felt. 'The missteps in your career that you've shared were no doubt distressing for those involved. But what if that father had never rung you? You would have been none the wiser to the pain and anguish that story caused the family. If journalists never get feedback, then nothing will ever change.'

James doesn't believe that even with feedback, many journalists would alter how they work. He believes empathetic journalists will act with empathy and that others will continue to act like cowboys. James signs off his email to me with one final thought:

'It was painful to have unkind and untrue things said about me. It's easier to read the news about other people, no doubt. But there's something I want people to understand and it's really important: life moves on.'

Four

The Things That Get You Through

In my second year as a journalist, I was sent to cover a demonstration in Brisbane organised by firefighters and their families. They were protesting about conditions and equipment after the deaths of two men fighting a housefire. I was looking for people to interview and there was a woman who seemed to be at the centre of the rally. She was wearing large sunglasses and holding a baby.

'What brings you to the march?' I asked as I sidled up.

'My husband was one of the firefighters who died,' she replied flatly.

I squawked, 'Oh,' and backed away as fast as I possibly could – even though a good journalist would have kept asking questions.

I was so floored and uncomfortable, I could think of absolutely nothing to say. I just wanted to get away from her. It was like the reaction of Walter Mikac's friend, Doug. I don't imagine that Doug was a bad person. He was almost certainly a good person, so devastated by what had happened to his dear friend that he couldn't bear to face him. Almost all of us know that feeling of helplessness, and the fear that we'll say or do the wrong thing.

When people find their lives turned upside down by unimaginable tragedy, they immediately discover that some friends and professionals seem to know exactly what to do and say while others have no idea. The world will divide into people who are helpful and people who are not.

If you do happen to be the person at the wrong end of the odds, what might get you through the worst days of your life? And for the rest of us, how can we get better at swallowing our own discomfort so that we are a comfort and not a hindrance?

Juliet Darling is the perfect name for the woman who knocks at my door. She is pretty and fine-featured with softly curling hair, just as one would imagine a Juliet, and it is rather darling that she is holding a bunch of daffodils for me. I feel ashamed, because I should be the one giving her something for coming here to face my questions about the most devastating events in her life.

I study Juliet's face closely, expecting grief to have carved sharp lines of anguish. Like my nightmare about Walter, somewhere in my subconscious I must believe that she will be outwardly marked by her suffering. It's not the case. She's one of those women whose face is gently creased in all the right places – crinkles at the corners of her eyes, fine lines on her forehead – so that she merely looks kindly. Juliet is dressed all in black but a thin red watchband peeps out of her sleeve, so subtly stylish that I suddenly form the opinion that red shoes are brazen.

I've attempted to make a chocolate and Chinese five-spice cake for us but the wretched thing wouldn't hold together when I removed it from the oven. I shovel it into the freezer in the hope it will somehow magically set, given I've messed up the baking. Juliet is polite enough not to comment when we sit at my dining table for almost two hours and still the promised cake doesn't appear.

I set down cups of tea and we begin by talking about her late partner, Nick Waterlow. In 1998, a mutual friend arranged for them to meet at a dinner party, and then again soon afterwards, alone in a bookshop café near Nick's workplace. Juliet was in her late forties and had a son, George, from an earlier relationship. Nick was fifteen years older with three children. Their matchmaking friend clearly had sound instincts, as Juliet and Nick felt an instant connection. Juliet remembers that their chatter was so comfortable and familiar, it felt more like a recollection than a conversation. They shared a love of the ridiculous and sometimes, late at night, they would scream so uncontrollably with laughter that a neighbour would ask the next day what had been so funny.

Nick Waterlow was a well-known figure in Sydney's art world. He had been the director of three Sydney Biennales and a mentor to countless students at the city's College of

Fine Arts. Born in London, Nick was an only child and had been sent to boarding school at the age of six. He told Juliet that from the moment he was exposed to art, he loved it with a deep passion. Art was his way of connecting with other people, drawing him out of himself. He always had a firm belief that he wasn't an artist; he knew that his talent lay in identifying interesting works of art and showing them: a curator. Nick was one of those people who made everyone feel they were the most important person in the room, and to him, in the moment he was speaking to them, they were. His warm nature made him loved by many.

There was one matter that was a source of profound stress and anxiety in the Waterlow family and it would come to engulf Juliet as well. Nick's youngest son, Antony, had been diagnosed with paranoid schizophrenia years earlier. He suffered from a delusion that his family had orchestrated a worldwide plot, 'an internet-based campaign of harassment', to persecute and destroy him. He believed that people could use 'secret technology' to control his thoughts and he experienced auditory hallucinations. From around the year 2000, Antony frequently demonstrated violent, aggressive and threatening behaviour, usually directed at his family. He repeatedly threatened to kill his father and siblings; he told Nick that he wanted to stab him.

Juliet was scared of Antony. Once, when he came to visit, she hid all the knives.

'Nick and I only had a very few arguments and they were always about this issue,' she says. 'I felt afraid. I felt, This is a dangerous situation. I couldn't explain quite why I felt it to that extent. But I think it was that I was an outsider and I could see his son's deranged thinking very clearly. And I thought, That's dangerous. I kept saying to Nick, "Don't walk on the main road with him. Don't eat anything in his house. Don't walk near the street with him, he could push you in front of a bus."'

'How did Nick react when you said things like that?' I ask.

'He listened.' Juliet pauses.

'Was he defensive because it was his son?' I probe.

'Yeah, a little bit,' she admits.

Antony had seen psychiatrists on and off but had always refused medication. He didn't meet the criteria to be scheduled (involuntarily admitted to a mental institution). At the time, Juliet was annoyed that Nick wasn't doing more to force the issue and protect himself, although she later learned that Nick had in fact gone to great lengths to try to help Antony. Nick didn't discuss the matter with Juliet – she thinks he was trying to protect her from further worry.

Despite Nick's efforts, by 2009 Juliet was living with a perpetual feeling of dread. She describes the atmosphere as being like the heavy, expectant feeling in the air before it rains, a sense that something is about to break.

'Every time I saw a police car, a fear would rise in my chest. I spent so many evenings lying awake, waiting for Nick to return, my breath caught in my throat.'

On the night of 9 November 2009, Juliet was doing just that, lying in bed reading. Nick and his daughter, Chloe, had invited Antony to Chloe's home for dinner. Nobody knows for certain the sequence of events that followed but at some point during the dinner, Antony armed himself with a knife and stabbed his sister and father to death. Chloe's daughter, a toddler, was also seriously injured. Nick died in the hallway, by the front door.

A neighbour heard the kerfuffle, including Nick's final words, directed at his son: 'I love you!' Later, the coroner who investigated the circumstances leading to their deaths would describe what happened as 'a love story, that like so many love stories, ends in tragedy'.

Around 10.30 pm, Juliet's phone rang and it was Nick's other son, Luke. He told her that two bodies had been found in a house in Randwick, the same suburb in which Chloe lived. Juliet knew in her gut that her worst fears had been realised. Not long afterwards, the police arrived. Juliet was terrified, as Antony had escaped and was nowhere to be found. She went into hiding at a friend's house and remained there until Antony was discovered in bushland and arrested, almost three weeks later. He pleaded not guilty to murder due to mental illness and was institutionalised indefinitely.

Nick's high profile on the art scene, and the horrifying nature of the crime and the violence of its circumstances, meant the deaths were front-page news for days.

'The world separated, in a way,' says Juliet. 'And people changed, in my view of them. The people who I thought were my friends were maybe not so close friends. Other ones were extraordinary. People revealed themselves differently. Maybe the people with courage came to the fore, and I saw their courage clearly, and maybe the people who were frightened, I saw their fear. I could see it in their faces and in their behaviour. I still feel that now.

But I have more compassion for the people who are frightened than I might have done before this, all this tragedy. I might have thought, Oh, that's bad behaviour, that's selfish. I might have judged them more. Now I feel their fear, and I feel more pity or sympathy for them.'

In the first days after Nick's death, Juliet was in a state of deep shock and terror. Looking back, she sees that two very different people were instrumental to her survival: a priest and a detective. Father Steve Sinn, a Jesuit who worked on the streets of Kings Cross, had previously worked at the same school Antony attended and had met Nick then. Detective Graham Norris, with the New South Wales homicide squad, was the lead investigator on the double murder case.

'If there were two people that were similar, it was the priest and the detective,' Juliet says. 'They stood back and listened and they asked questions and they waited for things to be revealed. They never presumed to know how I felt. They helped me because they trusted me. Well, they trusted maybe not me, but the whole endeavour. I got the feeling from the homicide detective, the priest, that I could have faith to trust myself.'

'Because they trusted that you were strong enough to carry on?' I ask.

'Yeah. They didn't give me a sense that I might not be able to. They never said, in words or gestures, Are you sure you can handle this?'

These two men fascinate me. How did they have such emotional intelligence at such an awful time? I ask Juliet to tell me more about them.

Father Steve appeared the day after Nick's death. Juliet recalls that one of the first things he did was take dead sunflowers out of a vase in the hallway and throw them away. He didn't ask if it was okay to do this, or even where the bin was. He just did it. The gesture is an incredibly memorable one to Juliet.

'That just represented everything to me. It showed me someone who valued life. Or maybe the gesture said, There is death but there is also life. It was such a simple, thoughtful act and I don't know, maybe the simpler and smaller, the better,' Juliet says. 'The big tragedy makes the small things more heightened and more vivid somehow. One gesture like that can change your life, in a way. It can open your heart to think that life is worth living. It doesn't sound quite true, but it is true for me.'

Father Steve helped Juliet organise Nick's funeral. Juliet remembers that when she went to his office, he began by saying to her, 'I don't know how you're going to manage.'

'Those were the kindest words,' she reflects. 'They acknowledged the depth of my pain and they didn't try to push my grief aside or hide it. There was no way to avoid grief and nobody else could do it for me.'

Superficially, 'I don't know how you're going to manage' sounds similar to the words Juliet feared somebody would say to her: 'Are you sure you can handle this?' But they're quite different. The second question contains an implied challenge – the situation must be handled and it's doubtful whether Juliet is up to it. The first statement applies no pressure and contains no expectation. With those words, the priest gave Juliet permission to feel overwhelmed; indeed, he was saying how could she not be? By offering his own bewildered humanity, Steve Sinn allowed Juliet hers.

Detective Norris was utterly unlike Father Steve in many ways, but the two men had one thing in common: empathy. Both could put themselves in another person's shoes and at the same time maintain the detachment necessary to carry out their work. Graham Norris would take a phone call at any time. Juliet once started sobbing in a post office and she rang the detective. He showed up to help her in a matter of minutes. At Nick's funeral, when Antony was still at large, Detective Norris subtly sidled up to Juliet before the service and murmured, 'You don't need to be afraid, you can't see us but we're everywhere.'

It was exactly what she needed to hear: it freed her to pay tribute to Nick and say goodbye without the gut-churning terror that Antony would appear.

Both men went with Juliet when she attended the morgue to view Nick's body. A counsellor named Jane Mowll met the group in the waiting room and began by telling Juliet what she could expect to see when she went inside. When she said Nick would feel cold to the touch, Juliet collapsed and began weeping uncontrollably.

Now, think for a moment what you would have done if you'd been there at the morgue with Juliet. I'm almost certain that I would have patted her and said, 'It's okay, Juliet, you don't have to go in if you don't want to.' That is not what the priest did. He stood, silently walked to the door of the viewing room and opened it. Then he helped lift Juliet to her feet and led her inside.

'I went in and when I saw Nick on the gurney, I just stopped crying straight away. It was suddenly this incredible peace, this amazing peace overtook me,' she says. 'Steve must have known. He must have known, now's the time to take her in, not to console or hug her.'

Even though Juliet saw Nick's body, in the weeks and months afterwards she had a great deal of difficulty coming to terms with the way he had died. She felt as if she were having a rolling bad dream while awake, replaying what she thought might have occurred. She had never read any of the media reports, so her state wasn't triggered by that. It was her imagination at work. It had concocted a film that played over and over again, the same sequence of shots: Antony rummages in the kitchen drawers. Chloe is busy making dinner and isn't watching. They argue and she doesn't see Antony pull a knife. Then Nick is struggling with Antony in the hallway as they wrestle towards the front door. Every muscle in Nick's face is strained and his eyes are full of terror. The final shot is a close-up of Antony's twisted face.

After two years of enduring this horror, Juliet decided she needed to see the crime scene photos.

'I thought that if I did, it might help me to see the reality of it as opposed to my imagination of it. Then it might stop the nightmare,' she says.

Once more, she visited the morgue, Father Steve by her side. Jane Mowll was again the person who met them. Juliet didn't know it at the time but she was in very good hands. Jane Mowll has a doctorate in psychology and her thesis was about viewings and how to sensitively handle them, in ways that give people the best chance of coping with death and loss.

'She was a wonderful woman,' Juliet says. 'She went into a lot of detail. She had a huge folder of documents, photographs and photocopies. She described each one before she handed it over. She described the watchband on the ground; now you're going to see another thing and another. And she did it in a very gentle way.'

'Did her descriptions help to neutralise the effect of what you were seeing?' I ask.

'I think so. It took out any emotion. She only described factually what you would see.'

There were many images. One showed a close-up of Nick's face, his eyes open and unseeing. Another showed him slumped on the ground, as if sleeping. There was a photo of Nick's wrist, which had been cut to the bone, followed by an image of his broken watch on the floor. Juliet saw the kitchen knife on the ground next to a ruler. She saw Nick's bloodied torso.

Juliet found the process of viewing the crime scene photos so helpful that she later gave a speech at a conference about forensic photography, describing the effect it had had on her:

I had been playing in my mind a fictionalised event for so long, that part of my consciousness had come to believe that I had actually 'been there'. And if I had been there, why hadn't I done more to help? Why was I a passive onlooker? To be able to see what had actually happened, and those images were far worse than my ideas of them, made me aware that

I couldn't have stopped the murders; I hadn't actually been there . . . maybe that was the moment when I could let them go. Looking at Nick's crime scene photos dissolved my fantasies. When I looked at the photographs, I felt my love for him and his love for me. I saw the emptiness of death and felt the fullness of love.

That speech made such an impact that it is quoted in *The Australasian Coroner's Manual* as best-case practice of how professionals should conduct viewings of crime scene photos and bodies in order to help traumatised relatives. Whether it was the sensitive way Jane Mowll assisted Juliet with those photographs, or the practical and thoughtful actions of Father Steve and Detective Norris, at the heart of what gave Juliet a reason to keep going was something very simple: kindness.

How *did* Father Steve and Detective Norris know exactly the right things to do? I wish I had that sort of confidence and wisdom. Were they just naturally empathetic? Or had their years of experience dealing with sudden tragedy and grief taught them how to act? I decided to track them both down to find out.

Father Steve was easy to find because he and Juliet had kept in touch. Detective Norris had retired and was trickier to locate. A police contact finally emailed me an old mobile phone number, and when I rang it around 7 pm one evening the former homicide cop picked up. We began an email correspondence while I made plans to catch up with Father Steve first.

Steve asked to meet at a place called Two Wolves, a Mexican-style cantina near Sydney University where you can order cheap tacos or enchiladas and wash them down with beers or margaritas. The bar is run by volunteers and is affiliated with the Jesuits. It's a not-for-profit social enterprise, raising money for disadvantaged communities in Thailand, Vietnam, Ecuador, Nepal and Sydney. It's not 'churchy' or square in any way, it's cool. There's a deer head mounted on the wall, a sombrero jauntily perched on it. Bright triangular flags hang from the roof, and the shutters are painted colourfully.

I see a man with short white hair, perhaps around seventy or so, sitting alone at a table. He looks trim, fit even, and wears a patterned shirt, as if he's going to a weekend barbecue. It fits the festive mood of the place quite well.

I introduce myself, take a seat and hit Steve with my first question: why did he want to be a priest?

He laughs. 'Well, you tell your story but you never know whether it's really the story,' he says.

Steve grew up in a large Catholic family in Victoria, with four brothers and four sisters. His father was a doctor and they were affluent, living in Toorak. His mother had beautiful taste and a wonderful eye, although she found caring for so many children a strain. When Steve was around seven, his oldest brother, Bill, started drinking and playing up. Steve remembers going to Mass on Sundays, packed into the car with the rest of his siblings, while his parents talked about Bill and how worried they were.

'I was in the back seat of the car and I remember picking up a holy picture – in those days there were holy pictures – and on the back of the picture, I read that if someone in the family becomes a priest, all of you will go to Heaven. And I thought, Well, I'll become a priest, everything will be alright,' he says. 'And I still don't feel it's much different. That's what a priest does. He holds up the pain, the anguish, the brokenness, the worries of our world to God on behalf of others. That's all I do.'

Steve joined the Jesuits in 1967 and he was ordained in 1979. The society of Jesuits dates back centuries, and its priests and brothers are known for their deep commitment to social justice and education. Jesuits are particularly motivated by Jesus' teachings on helping the poor, the marginalised and the disadvantaged. Steve has spent most of his ministry in Sydney's Kings Cross, working with the homeless, mentally ill and drug-addicted. I asked the prime minister, Malcolm Turnbull, if he knew of Steve, given that his electorate takes in the Cross. He did, and he described the priest's work on the streets as 'saintly'. Another work contact of mine, a judge who is no longer a practising Catholic but spent six years of his youth living with the Jesuits, also knew Steve. When he was desperately conflicted about leaving the Jesuits, it was Steve who counselled him that it was okay to go. Like the prime minister, the judge also considers Steve Sinn to be genuinely Christlike.

One thing I very quickly learn about Steve is that I don't think the way he does. I have come to the interview with a series of questions about how he does his job. He doesn't think that he has a job.

'Juliet was so touched that you arrived at her house and the first thing you did was take away some dead flowers,' I say. 'In a practical sense, in your line of work, how do you know what to do that will help?'

Steve pauses, then says, 'I don't even remember that. I don't know if I do know what somebody needs practically. No, I don't think I do know, actually.'

'In your job,' I say, 'are you all the time listening and observing and trying to work out what to do? Or are you talking to God in your head? What is the process?'

There's another long pause. There is nothing hurried about Father Steve. When I listen to the recording of our conversation, it's peppered with pauses of five to ten seconds – very long silences when you think of a regular chat. But Steve is entirely comfortable with sitting silently. It alarms me at first, but after a while it's quite pleasant to sit together without saying anything, restful to not have to rush to think of what to say next.

'You see, Leigh,' Steve says, 'I was ordained for this. I'm not working, I'm not acting, I'm just myself. I'm not acting the shepherd, I *am* the shepherd; that's what ordination is. I believe when I go into a situation, others know that because I'm a priest, God is with them. They're not abandoned, their suffering is their entrance into His suffering and resurrection.'

'But what if the person's not religious? What if they don't believe in God?' I ask.

'Oh, I don't *say* that to people!' he exclaims with a laugh. 'If I'm there, they know. We are His presence to one another, human beings. God doesn't dwell out there –' Steve gestures away from us – 'we are bearers of the divine to one another. It's sacred, suffering is sacred. We don't want it. We can't avoid it. But you need to have someone with you. It's just being present, it's accompanying rather than helping. There is a deep truth in that, accompanying.'

'In your role, being like a shepherd —' I begin again.

'I'm not like a shepherd, I *am* a shepherd,' Steve interrupts and we both laugh. I really am having a hard time getting my head around this. I don't see any sheep. Therefore to me, he is not a shepherd.

'It's like you are a mother,' he says. 'Your work is a journalist but you are a mother; you're not working as a mother, you're not acting like a mother, you are a mother. I am a shepherd.'

I finally think I get it. It's complicated, though, because I don't dwell in this religious world and I'm struggling. I suddenly think, Oh dear, I've been calling him Steve the whole time. Should I be calling him Father Steve? Or maybe the correct etiquette is Father Sinn? But somehow Steve doesn't strike me as the sort of person who cares what he's called.

'Leigh,' he says, 'when I was a young priest, one of the Jesuits who was a very flawed human being but still a mentor, he said people are often afraid to visit someone in hospital. But he said, it's not about you, it's about them, forget about you. It doesn't matter what I say or do, it's not about me. It's about that person. And so, you know, if you're inadequate, you say the wrong thing, so what? If they have a go at you, so what? Fine. Just be there. It's them that's the focus. I don't have a pathway or a lifeline, I just believe in people. And I believe in time.'

I ask him about accompanying Juliet to the morgue and taking her into the viewing room to see Nick's body, even though she had broken down outside.

'It was such a big experience for somebody,' I say. 'How did you know that what she needed in that moment was not to be consoled but that she had to go in?'

Steve pauses again for a long time, then says, 'I've had a lot of experience with people who are dead, with their bodies. Our bodies are everything. If you love someone, you have to be next to them, you have to have time with the body. I would never, ever want to be apart from the body. I think we've taken it away too much, the funeral people take over. No! Let people bury their own!'

'Do you think it helps people to go through the process and be intimately involved?'

'Yes! Of course! Of course!' It's the most emphatic Steve has been about anything. 'Keep the body at home! Put it on the dining table! Let the kids sleep under the table, paint the coffin, decorate it. Eat! When my brother died, we had fights over the coffin, drinking whiskey. I remember one brother pounding Bill's coffin: "Oh you bastard!" It was our lives. We carried the coffin, we filled in the hole. I used to work in the garden as a boy with my father and I dug the hole to put his plants in and filled in the hole. In the end, we put Dad into the ground and I helped my brothers fill in the hole. We need to do it ourselves.'

'Why do you think it helps to have that involvement?' I ask.

'It's our responsibility, it's not to help. It's enabling us to grieve, it's enabling us to go through it together. Otherwise it's taken away and *whoosh*, it's gone, and you can't grieve. You've got to feel, you've got to touch, you've got to be there!' Steve is passionate.

He reaches into his bag to pull out something to show me. It's an old yellowing newspaper clipping. The caption reads, 'Devastation: a woman in despair at the site of one of the blasts near the Turkey–Syrian border.' The photograph with it shows a woman standing in a pile of rubble. She has her arms open to the sky and she is wailing, her head thrown back.

'I pray in front of that,' Steve tells me as I look at it. 'That's a wonderful photo of the pain of our world. I don't know if she's lost relatives or what's blown up. You have a substance to your life if you've felt pain. You've got understanding, that's where compassion is. It makes you a deeper, richer human being.'

'How do you stand to be around the suffering all the time, though?' I ask.

'Well, I got burned out,' Steve confesses. 'I was eighteen years in the Cross. I don't like that term "burned out", actually. But I needed a change. I was emotionally so exposed there. It's like a bombsite, with people walking around; you get these waves of people just not coping all that well.'

'So what did you do when you burned out?'

'I needed some space. I got into a car and went driving on my own, living in country hotels. Bourke, Brewarrina. I was about sixty-five, I'd got to that stage of my life where I thought, Well I've got twenty years left. What do I want to do? I want to live with people coming out of prison, I want to break bread and share our lives in community. I saw that as a real need.'

And so that's what Steve does now. He lives with prisoners transitioning back into the community after they're released from Bathurst Correctional Complex, and other nearby prisons.

'I'm a Jesuit, so I belong to a community. I have a life. I'm not a homeless person, I'm not addicted to drugs. I'm claimed by my Jesuit companions, we have a structured community life where we pray together and eat together and share our lives.'

'Does that replenish you?'

'Yeah. I also spend a couple of hours in the morning doing things for myself. I used to get up at 4.30 and go and swim at Bondi and come back and pray. Prayer is very important. I suppose it's just like shedding, it's just letting go. I just sit and breathe and count. I count my heartbeat.'

'The jargon is about "living in the moment",' I venture. 'Are you like that? Do you worry about the future, do you have regrets about the past?'

For once, Steve doesn't pause. 'I wish I wasn't such a coward. All my life, still I'm a coward,' he says.

There follows the longest silence of our conversation. It lasts about twenty seconds, mostly because I am absolutely dumbstruck that this man, *this man*, eighteen years on the streets of Kings Cross, planning to spend the rest of his life helping ex-prisoners, considers himself a coward. I finally manage to splutter out a response.

'Steve, a lot of people would look at what you do and say it would be the least cowardly thing they could ever imagine – sitting with people when they're experiencing moments of intense suffering, going with them to say goodbye to the dead bodies of people they love. That's not cowardly.'

He thinks for a while. 'No. But I do admire people who speak up. People who sit in a tree to stop it being cut down. People who speak out against how we treat refugees. They're not cowards. I haven't been hit, I haven't been shot, I haven't been criticised. In fact, people think I'm wonderful!'

I think he's quite wonderful too, I must admit. I find it hard to process some of what he says, but there's something about him that makes me wish I could spend more time with him. Steve makes me feel like I could be a better person.

When I meet Graham Norris a few weeks later, he's easier for me to 'get', because I have met many police officers over the years and his 'type' is more familiar to me. The first thing to note about this former homicide detective is that he's off-the-charts likeable. Within about five minutes of meeting him, you think, I'd love to have a beer with this bloke. Graham is tall with a shaved head and a long, full grey beard that reminds me of a bushranger. He has a broad Australian accent, a straightforward way of speaking and a larrikin sense of humour. He tells me about his old boss in the force, the amusingly named – and, I might add, highly respected – Inspector Hans Rupp (Get it? A police officer named Hands Are Up.) Rupp kept showing up at daily briefings during a large-scale manhunt after a double homicide declaring, 'I'm 100 per cent certain [the suspect] is dead, we just have to find the body,' until one day, the suspect was sighted withdrawing cash at an ATM, and when Rupp arrived at that day's briefing, he opened with, 'I'm fairly certain the suspect is alive.'

Graham was a late starter in the police, joining the force in 1997 at the age of thirty-five after a career in sales. He had always wanted to be a policeman but his parents were opposed to such a dangerous job, so he'd taken a different path to keep them happy. Over time, though, he couldn't let his dream go and so, thinking better late than never, he headed to the New South Wales Police Academy. His first assignment after graduation was general duties at the station in Mount Druitt, a fairly depressed area in Sydney's south-west.

'It was the happiest I've ever been,' Graham says. 'You never knew what was going to happen. Every day was a blank canvas. I loved the variety, the intensity, I really liked the physical aspect of it. It was good, it was a challenge.'

In 2004, he moved into the State Crime Command, where he specialised in child protection and sex crimes, and four years later he joined the homicide squad.

'Often,' he says, 'there's an intrigue with people and the police and what they do. I mean, there's a thousand cop shows on telly, people are interested in it. And they always ask, "What's the worst murder you've ever been to?" They're all bad.'

'When you went to homicide, did you have any fear about things like being around dead bodies and going to crime scenes and seeing foul stuff?' I ask.

'The only thing I was a bit apprehensive about was seeing the post-mortems, because at that time, I'd have to lie down if I was going to get a needle,' Graham says (while I'm thinking, Wow, big call to move to homicide!). 'You have to go to post-mortems in the cops and you can't go, "I'm gonna spew," or, "I can't watch this." It's just a fact of life, you gotta do it. It's really crucial to the investigation to find out certain things. And so once I got that in my head, I didn't mind, it was just part of the job. Seeing dead people, you see some horrendous things, but you can look at it and go, "Bloody hell, that's nasty." It's part of the job. But it's no good saying, "I want to work in homicide," or "I want to work in sex crimes," if the thought of going to a murder scene or speaking to a sexual assault victim is too much for you.'

'What about having to deal with families at that really heightened period when they've just discovered somebody they love has been killed?'

'That's challenging, there's no doubt about it. Going to tell somebody that. Death messages are always hard.'

'Do you get any training for that?'

'Oh yeah, at the academy, you get lots of things. But how can I put it? You get taught a lot at the academy and then they put you in the real world and you start learning.'

'If you had to go and see somebody and break that sort of news, what was your general approach?'

'I found over time the best way was to be fairly direct about it. When you're going to do your first one, you don't wanna say the words, you know; you're a bit afraid about how they're gonna respond. But the reality is, if you get it out early and clearly, then you deal with the emotions that come after that,' he says.

'And is there any predictability to the way people respond to news like that?'

'No. You get everything. I've had somebody, you wake them up, two in the morning, you know, your father's dead, or your brother's dead, and they're like, "Mate, you've made my day, come in and have a coffee, you want some biscuits?"'

I gasp. 'Wow!'

'And you're like, "Nah, we're good, thanks,"' says Graham, making an alarmed face and backing-away motions with his hands.

'I had one,' he goes on, 'I don't know what nationality she was, she didn't speak a whole lot of English – her son had committed suicide and I was telling her and she's got to her knees and she starts punching me and she's whacked me right in the boys! I'm going, *Euffff*.' Graham makes a strangled noise and has me cracking up again.

In 2009, Graham found himself officer-in-charge on the Waterlow murders. We get to talking about the day of Nick Waterlow's funeral and how he helped Juliet by telling her that she was protected.

'I've heard what was going through her mind. What was going through yours?' I ask him.

'It was stressful for us as well,' Graham admits straight up. 'We didn't know where he [Antony] was. He was clearly dangerous, he's murdered two people and nearly killed a little girl along the way. While it was unlikely that he would attack at a big event like a funeral, you don't know. What if he comes charging in? So you've got to prepare for the worst.'

'What would you have done if he'd shown up?' I ask.

'Depending what he did or what his actions were, we would have had to respond accordingly,' he says, in a bit of classic copper-speak.

'Were you guys armed?'

'Oh yeah, yeah, always.'

'What gave you the insight to think, I'm going to have a reassuring word to Juliet? Did you know she was scared that he might show up, or did you just intuit it?'

'I think that was ever-present with Juliet, that fear that he was going to turn up somewhere, that he was going to leap out and attack her. You're trying to reassure her but we don't have crystal balls. You've got to try to placate someone's fears and nerves as best you can without being dismissive or insensitive to what they're saying, because it's 100 per cent real to them.'

Until I contacted Graham out of the blue, he had no idea that he'd been so instrumental to Juliet's survival.

'It's a nice feeling,' he tells me. 'I was talking to my wife about it and I said I don't even remember some of the things Juliet says I did, and my wife said maybe that's just cos it's what you're always doing, day to day, and it wasn't out of the ordinary for you to treat someone that way. For me, it was, This is a family member of a victim, I've gotta look after her, that's my job.'

'What do you mean when you say you felt you had to look after people, that it's your job?'

'To me, it was to put them in cottonwool because this is a long process they're entering into. The legal process is going to be counted in years, not months, and for them, it's a lifetime of change. I always felt a strong responsibility, a heavy responsibility, to look after these people. You'd love to be able to say, "I'm gonna get you the outcome that you want, you'll be happy at the end of all of this," but that just doesn't happen. So if the person that I'm looking after, if we get to the end of whatever process, and it's not the outcome they wanted or expected, they might feel disappointed in that, but at least they won't feel disappointed in the way I've looked after them.'

All through our interview, the thing that strikes me most about Graham is that only rarely does he call anyone a victim. He calls them 'the person I was looking after', in a way that seems to me unmediated. He seems genuinely driven to care for others. He tells me about a case of which he's particularly proud – the successful prosecution of a violent serial rapist who targeted sex workers.

'This group of women, they hated the cops, they had never had anybody who would spend time with them and look after them,' Graham says. 'One of them lived in this horrendous housing commission unit in Redfern and she was told she was being evicted. So she's rung me in tears, What am I gonna do? So I rang the guy from the housing department and said blah blah, This is who I am, she's a victim in a rather serious matter, it would be really helpful if you could just keep her there. And he's gone, Yeah mate, no worries, and she thought I'd turned water into wine. And over time, the women built enough trust in me that they would come to court. I got the relationship strong enough that I could get them there. And that resulted in the fellow getting over twenty years for it.'

I listen to Graham and I think, This is a really good man sitting here. Drug-addicted sex worker or educated middle-class woman like Juliet, he sees the humanity in all of them and treats them in ways that respect their dignity.

Like almost every other person to whom I speak in the death business, Graham hates the word 'closure'.

'I've never felt comfortable when people say closure. Their normal is shattered. I tried to talk to people about, "This is your new normal. We've got to find a way of making life with this new set of circumstances." You can't get them back their old life,' he says.

The great tragedy of Graham's own story is that this wonderfully wise bloke who was so clearly fantastic at his job is no longer a police officer. He didn't burn out or get PTSD, he injured his back during a training exercise in 2010, and by 2014 it was so bad the police medically discharged him. He now lives with chronic pain.

'The difficulty for me is that there's reminders every day. You turn the telly on, there's cops on the news. You see a job, somebody's been murdered, it's like, That's my team. I'm still wrapping my head around the retirement word. It's difficult. I loved my job, I just loved going to work. I don't wanna say I was good at it, but I felt I was okay at it,' he says.

I know the loss is partly Graham's but I can't help but think the bigger loss is ours, not having such a caring person in frontline policing. It's impossible to think that Juliet Darling was in any way lucky in the situation in which she found herself, but she was certainly extremely fortunate in having Graham Norris and Steve Sinn on either side, holding her up.

Like the priest and the detective, some people are blessed with instinctive emotional intelligence. They just seem to know the right things to say and do at times of grief and loss. Undoubtedly, experience helps too; the nature of their jobs taught Graham and

Steve how to behave. Most of us probably aren't so adept around the bereaved. We bumble about, sometimes making things worse, as Juliet and Walter found. Emotional incompetence isn't limited to individuals, either. If you've ever spent time in hospitals or courts, or rung a bank when a loved one has died, you'll know that institutions can be particularly bad at compassion. Navigating an impersonal bureaucracy can seem bewildering at the best of times and downright heartless at the worst. Imagine if we could get big, lumbering bureaucracies to act more like Steve and Graham. Is it possible? What if we could institutionalise that type of kindness?

The legal profession has made a big effort to do something like that during the past twenty years. It's called therapeutic jurisprudence. The term came into common use in the 1990s, after it was coined by an American academic, David Wexler. He believed that the law should try to aid the recovery of people caught in the system, that it should work with other professions, such as psychiatry, social work and criminology. Under this approach, lawyers and judges are encouraged to bear in mind that the law is a social force with consequences for individual psychological wellbeing. Those considerations never trump legal obligations, they fit in wherever they can alongside. The law still comes first.

Every day, judges and lawyers witness the impact of the legal system on the people who land in it, often through no fault of their own. Numerous studies in Australia and overseas have catalogued the ways in which the justice process causes stress and trauma. Its impersonality can be cruel – form letters sent by coroners, names spelt incorrectly in correspondence.

Courts frequently grind through cases very slowly, prolonging the agony of those waiting for answers. The experience of appearing as a witness can be troubling. The inquisitorial nature of a trial or inquest can make any witness, even those with nothing to hide, feel as if they're being judged or attacked. I saw this at the Lindt Café inquest. Blameless witnesses sometimes seemed defensive and perplexed, even angered, when barristers challenged their recollections. People can step down from the witness box feeling humiliated and confused about what has just happened to them.

For observers, especially the families of people at the centre of inquests or trials, the process can be even more traumatic. They may hear distressing information they've never heard before, have to listen to their loved one described in ways that are foreign to them, or hear and see evidence of that person's final moments. They may be seated a few metres from somebody they believe caused the death. When evidence is presented, the family may feel judged for decisions they did or didn't make, when often they already feel guilt about what has happened. The loss of privacy in having intimate personal matters publicly exposed can be excruciating. And if the case is a high-profile one, the family and friends may find themselves besieged by journalists and television cameras every time they enter and leave the court precinct.

A particularly confronting experience for many bereaved is the autopsy process. In 2001 in Australia, major reforms were made to forensic practices after investigations revealed that body organs had been retained for use in research without consent. The head of the Glebe morgue in New South Wales was forced to stand down after an inquiry found that more than 25,000 organs had been removed without permission from the next of kin. They were kept in hospitals, universities and museums. The inquiry also uncovered evidence of looting of the deceased's belongings, along with experimentation on bodies for research purposes, including stabbing and applying blunt force (supposedly to give forensic researchers insight into how certain injuries might present). The NSW Department of Health had to deal with dozens of anguished families hoping to trace lost organs and stolen possessions. A similar scandal unfolded in the United Kingdom, prompting the same outrage and reform there.

These revelations acted as a wake-up call to authorities on the need for change, but they did little to ease the fears of people about what might be happening to the dead bodies of loved ones behind closed doors.

Once you accept that the pursuit of justice can cause people further pain, how do you apply therapeutic jurisprudence to mitigate that harm as much as possible? It doesn't have to be elaborate. The way that Jane Mowll talked Juliet through the viewing of Nick's crime scene photos is one example. Or it can be as simple as allowing a family to rearrange their seating in a courtroom to be closer together, or asking them how they would like the coroner to refer to the deceased. It can be allowing them to display a photograph in the courtroom, even though it serves no forensic purpose. It can be double-checking the spelling of a name before a court notification is sent out. It might be granting a relative permission to make a statement in a hearing so that they feel they've had a say – something Juliet did.

At the NSW Coroner's Court, a wonderful, sensible young woman named Jane Gladman is on staff full-time to liaise with the families of the deceased. She helps with anything they need, on one occasion rifling through human waste in the morgue to find a placenta that a grieving mother wanted. At the time of writing, Jane is lobbying to have a dog allowed into the court building: research shows that animals can be a source of comfort to troubled souls, and Jane thinks it's worth trying.

Therapeutic jurisprudence is not an uncontroversial idea and not everyone in the legal profession subscribes to it. Why should courts be bothered with any of this? Isn't that the job of psychologists and social workers? A court's mission is to dispense justice, not to fret about the emotional lives of participants and interested parties. The law values dispassionate reason above all else; it is the realm of fact, logic and intellect, not emotion, instinct and subjectivity. Asking judges to consider the mental health of witnesses and families, and to perhaps even change court processes to better accommodate them, is surely asking for trouble.

Yet for all the law's emphasis on reason, the tales that play out in front of judges frequently have at their core some of the most irrational passions imaginable – rage, jealousy, lust, grief. Courts are places where humanity is distilled to its most raw. The idea that the law can exist in an emotionless vacuum is patently nonsense. If we believe that courts exist to preserve our society's values and to protect all of us, then surely caring for the wellbeing of those who pass through their doors – or at least avoiding further harm to them – is part of the law's obligation.

Critics of therapeutic jurisprudence do raise valid concerns, especially the potential compromise to the ability of judges to remain impartial once their minds are open to considerations beyond the law. Many legal officers are confronted with death, often in horrific circumstances, on a daily basis, and they need to ensure that their emotions don't undermine reasoned judgement. It can be hard to maintain the necessary detachment once you start putting yourself in somebody else's shoes. It's one of the reasons the NSW Coroner's Court employs Jane Gladman. She deals closely with the families and their needs so the coroner can remain at arm's length.

Cases of suicide are known to cause judges to struggle against their personal feelings. Several Australian and British studies have found that coroners will generally resist declaring a death a suicide unless they absolutely must. The research shows that this is partly because coroners are aware that many people still strongly believe there's a stigma around suicide. Certain religions consider it shameful. Moreover a lot of suicides, such as those by drug overdose or drowning, also lend themselves to uncertainty. You may think, Well, what harm does it do if a coroner resists labelling a death a suicide if that will comfort the family involved? Potentially quite a bit of harm, is the answer. Governments make policy decisions and allocate resources based on official statistics. Under-reporting of suicides affects the amount of attention given to the problem. Australian authorities already know that suicide is a serious epidemic, but disturbingly, it's almost certainly worse than the numbers reveal, due to under-reporting.

Even noting the potential downside of therapeutic jurisprudence, it's hard to see how its goal is not a good one. Courts regularly come in for heavy criticism in the media, sometimes justly, often unfairly: they're supposedly biased in favour of criminals, sentences are too lenient, the proceedings are insufficiently transparent, judges are activists . . . This emphasis on the negative causes some in the community to feel cynical about the justice system, even though our society would crumble if we lost respect for the law and faith in the institutions that uphold it. If citizens see that courts are making an effort to meet the personal needs of those who walk through their doors, then surely it can only build public confidence.

In Juliet Darling's experience, the principles of therapeutic jurisprudence and their sensitive application by Jane Mowll at the morgue helped her come to terms with her terrible experience in a way that nothing else had. Combined with the personal kindness of the priest and the detective, it was instrumental in her eventual recovery. What made the difference to Juliet was that the professionals all viewed her first and foremost as a fellow human being, not just a case number.

Three years after Nick Waterlow was murdered, Juliet Darling suffered another truly shattering blow: her 26-year-old son, George, died on a building site in remote bushland. After lifting a heavy beam into a roof vault, he lay down, let out a sigh and then his heart stopped. An autopsy couldn't find any apparent cause for his heart failure.

Father Steve Sinn celebrated the funeral Mass. The front of the program for the service shows a white horse, saddled, its head bowed as it munches grass under the vast branches of an old tree. A dear little boy, perhaps ten or eleven, sits on the horse, but not on the saddle. He perches on the flank, his arms folded nonchalantly, facing backwards with his legs dangling amongst the tail. He gazes directly into the camera. He's not smiling, but nor does he look challenging or defiant. He looks simply as if he's declaring, *I am*.

Juliet delivered the eulogy. She spoke of what a free spirit George was, how even at a very young age he had no difficulty with the concept of letting go. Juliet recalled an event from long before, when she and George visited Atlanta.

'An old black man came up out of the darkness and gave George a yellow flower. George took it as graciously as if it were a gift. Then, when the old man demanded money, George, with the gentlest of smiles, took a step forward and offered it back, letting it go with the same grace and ease he had in receiving it. That's how he lived. He took things as they came and he let them be,' Juliet told the gathered mourners.

Life has forced Juliet to learn to let go too. After the agony of losing Nick, it was beyond painful to say goodbye to George.

'I remember someone saying, "Juliet, people die all the time,"' she tells me as she starts to cry. 'Yes, but not everyone in your whole life who you've loved.'

'With your son dying so soon after Nick, has the grief been different?' I ask her. I feel quite loathsome putting these questions but I know that even though it hurts, she doesn't mind answering. If she hadn't made that explicitly clear from the start, I wouldn't ask.

'The pain is similar. My son was so happy and such a joyful person, so much at peace with himself, that he just seemed like he was taken. I feel him inside me more. Nick is a different person, so I feel more bereft and empty and alone by his departure. Somehow, my son has been enfolded into me and I can hear him saying, "Come on Mum, you'll love again."'

I tell Juliet how upset I was to learn that her son had died. 'I know this is a form of magical thinking, but when you emailed me that your son had died, I just felt, Oh no, that's so unfair because Juliet has already had her one, big, awful thing happen. Why has another big, awful thing happened to her? I felt indignant, even though I know rationally that Nick dying could not protect you from other bad things happening.'

'Yes,' Juliet replies simply.

I blather on like a fool for a while because it's so sad, and unlike Steve or Graham, I have nothing useful or comforting to say. Finally I deliver the wrecked cake from the freezer and attempt to slice it. It hasn't set as I'd hoped and so it slowly oozes all over Juliet's plate like my clumsy words are gushing all over the room.

'I'm a very sceptical person now,' Juliet says. 'Death, for me, has really thrown me into this new, much more sceptical, but I hope not cynical, state.'

'What are you sceptical of?' I ask.

'Sceptical of ideas like "things will work out for the best if you're a good person". The reality is, some things do and some things don't.'

'All those truisms – like hard work pays off? Not really,' I say.

'No, you can work really hard and go bust. Someone who doesn't work very hard at all wins the lottery or is given an inheritance out of the blue from a friend.'

'How about "What doesn't kill me makes me stronger"? Does it?' I ask.

'Not necessarily,' she says. 'It might really mean you can't leave the house. They are ideas that are contemptuous somehow of the real world and the facts. Before I experienced the death of somebody I truly loved, I thought certain things had to happen or would happen for a reason. Like a plot. But I see now that there are no plots. I feel that I've been plunged into the truth of existence with all its contradictions and surprises.'

We eat our cake and drink more tea. Like Walter, Juliet is not an angry or bitter person in spite of the incredible weight of grief and loss she carries.

'You've trusted me by telling me your story,' I say. 'What do you hope somebody reading it would take away?'

Juliet thinks for a moment. What she says has echoes of Michael Spence's experience.

'That in pain, there's also joy. You can't be in the presence of just one thought, that life is good, or life is bad, or life is sad. There's all these things. And there are so many good people in the world, actually, so much kindness. It's everywhere.'

Five

A New Normal

Like Juliet, everyone who experiences a sudden tragedy must adapt to a new normal, to use Graham Norris's expression. A major crisis forces a person to reassess their beliefs about how the world works against the reality of what has happened, and the original views won't always survive. It's no simple thing to mentally and emotionally accommodate a life-changing blindside. Why do some people seem to recover better than others?

Few people have had their attitude to life tested as sharply as Stuart Diver, one of the most famous disaster survivors in Australia. In 1997, he was the only person to be pulled alive from a massive landslide at Thredbo in the Snowy Mountains. Eighteen people, including his wife Sally, died when two ski lodges were destroyed. Stuart spent sixty-five hours underground, on the brink of death himself, until his rescue. The experience was so harrowing that it's tempting to once again embrace magical thinking and assume that Thredbo must have fulfilled Stuart's lifetime allotment of suffering. Sadly, as for Louisa and Juliet, life had another breathtaking twist in store. In 2015, Stuart's second wife, Rosanna, died from breast cancer, leaving him alone with their four-year-old daughter Alessia.

'I know people think this,' Stuart tells me when we meet, 'they haven't said it right to me, but they think, Who's going to sign up to be the third Mrs Diver? I think the same. God, this next person who comes along, they have to deal with all this.'

Stuart is forty-seven, a strikingly good-looking man with wavy grey hair, a trim physique, and a tanned face that suggests a lot of time spent outdoors. He puts on the jug when I arrive at his cottage in Thredbo and we share tea in his living room. Alessia is outside playing with her cousin but every inch of the house shouts her presence – toys, sneakers, drawings, and other little-girl tchotchkes are scattered everywhere.

When you read just now that Stuart Diver had lost two wives, did you for a split second think some variation of, He must be jinxed? If so, that's your brain humming away involuntarily, trying to impose cause and effect. It's also yet another example of the way the mind misleads. Stuart Diver is not jinxed, although he has undoubtedly been unlucky. Stuart lost one wife in an incredibly rare, freak event, something for which nobody could possibly blame Stuart Diver himself. Once the landslide was in his past and he remarried, his odds of becoming a widower reset. Unfortunately, Stuart then had the misfortune to lose his second wife to something comparatively common, breast cancer. For women aged 45–54, breast cancer is the number-one killer, annually claiming one life in 4066 in Australia. It was unusual for Stuart Diver to lose his first wife in a landslide but it was sadly ordinary to lose his second to cancer.

You might be thinking, Hang on, I still reckon losing two wives by the age of forty-four is pretty weird. Well, you're right about that, it *is* unlucky to be twice widowed by that age. In the 2011 census of the Australian population (the most current at the time of writing), there were more than 8 million adult men. Among them, only 6239 men of Stuart's age or younger were widowers. Being widowed twice by age forty-four is a little like flipping a coin. The loss of Stuart's first wife neither reduced nor increased his chance of losing his second, in the same way that tossing ten heads does not reduce or increase the chances of tossing a head the eleventh time. From the moment you throw the eleventh coin in the air, the odds of heads are fifty-fifty. Ten heads in a row does not cause a tail to arrive next. The loss of Sally and the loss of Rosanna were their own, discrete events with no causal link between them, certainly not the tie to Stuart Diver. Nonetheless, like the tossing of ten heads, the more of the same result in a row, the rarer the experience.

Let's think about the future now and assume that next year, Stuart will meet and marry the third Mrs Diver. We already know that his background is no shield against the poison darts of fate; a happily-ever-after ending is not guaranteed. We also know that a tragic past does not make him more susceptible to a tragic future. The third Mrs Diver will be on her own path, independent of Stuart's history, and so she need not have any special fear because of her association with him.

But what about Stuart himself: what are his chances of being widowed a third time? Is having another relationship worth the risk? Let's assume that Stuart marries somebody the same age as him. Of every hundred Australian women aged forty-seven right now, 2.1 of them will die during the next decade, mostly likely from breast cancer, suicide or lung cancer. Even if we add some assumptions about the risks to the third Mrs Diver's longevity based specifically on being married to Stuart – she may have an elevated chance of dying in a skiing accident compared to the average Australian woman; she may have a higher chance of dying in a car or plane accident, because Stuart enjoys frequent travel and she's likely to travel with him – she still does not have an elevated risk of dying simply because his first two wives died. There is no jinx. In fact, the next person most likely to be bereaved in the Diver household would be the third Mrs Diver herself, because the average Australian woman lives a couple of years longer than the average Australian man. The odds favour Stuart dying before his third wife.

Probability and statistics being complicated matters, it took me more than two weeks to crunch the numbers given above, with the help of Michael Wilson at the Australian Bureau of Statistics. When I finally wrote those paragraphs in a way that seemed to make sense, I emailed them to him to check.

'That is a perfect piece of logic,' Michael replied, 'but even with all that work, I bet people will read it and go, Yeah, well, I still think Stuart Diver's jinxed.'

Annoyingly, he's probably right. Perhaps the explanation that somebody is doomed, as silly as that is, is simpler for our brain to handle than a complex calculation involving many steps of logic.

Stuart has his own rational explanation of why the idea that he's jinxed is nonsense.

'If you try to read too much into a tragedy, and you think, I'm jinxed, or, This is bad karma, or whatever, then you're reading way too much into yourself. You're making yourself way more important than you are,' Stuart says. He tells me that he's 'just a fortunate guy in that building that the eight thousand tonnes fell down on, and every heavy bit missed me. That's it. There's nothing else to be read into it. Then I'm the most fortunate guy in the world because I met Rosanna, I got to share sixteen years of my life with her, we had an unbelievable time. She got cancer, as a lot of people do, and she tragically died. But that's got nothing to do with *me*. That's just what happens in life.'

There would be few Australians old enough to have watched television in 1997 who don't remember Stuart Diver's extraordinary survival after the Thredbo landslide. It was one of the first rolling news broadcasts on Australian TV. In 1997 Stuart was a 27-year-old-ski instructor working and living at Thredbo with his wife Sally. At around 11.30 pm on 30 July, they were woken when their apartment started moving and shaking. Everything was crashing down; the windows smashed inwards, showering them with glass in their bed. As they sat up in shock, the walls and roof caved in as well. Sally was screaming that she couldn't move and that she had no feeling from her waist down. Stuart had fared better and had a bit of wiggle room.

Stuart and Sally didn't know it at the time of course, but what had caused their building to crumble was the collapse of the Alpine Way, the main road through Thredbo. Heavy rain, melting snow and unstable terrain underneath the road had fatally weakened it. Two thousand square metres of liquefied soil and a massive torrent of water took seconds to ram two ski lodges together, including the one in which Stuart and Sally lived.

As the couple tried to get their bearings in the dark, the cavern in which they were trapped began to fill with freezing, filthy water. Both began to scream in pain and terror. I can't capture the horror of what happened next any more graphically than Stuart does himself in his own book:

I'm holding Sally's face. I can't shift the bedhead off her; it's not budging; I'm trying, oh god, I'm trying to move it. The water's absolutely freezing – it takes my breath away. The water keeps rising. I put my hand over Sal's mouth. I've got to stop the water getting in. It's rising, rising. It's useless. I can feel the water seeping between my fingers, filling her mouth. I've got to stop the water. Please, I've got to stop the water. It floods in, I can't stop it. She's gurgling, drowning as her lungs fill up. My hand is still over her mouth. I can feel her face, contorted. The screaming has stopped . . . I feel the life drain out of my wife's body . . . she goes limp. I can't see her face but I know it's a mask of sheer terror . . . I take my hand away.

The water kept rising until it was lapping at the bottom of Stuart's chin. He was pressed into a tiny air pocket near the collapsed roof. Just as he thought he was about to drown, the water began to recede. During the many hours until his rescue, the same thing kept happening: water would fill the cavity until Stuart thought it would engulf him, then at the last moment it would flow away. At times he was suicidal and contemplated letting go, sliding into the water and ending his physical and emotional pain.

Outside, a massive recovery effort involving more than a thousand people was under way, but the focus was on body retrieval, not rescue. Nobody expected to find any survivors. Stuart could hear the noise of workers above ground but they couldn't hear him. A little after 5.30 am on 2 August, two and a half days into his ordeal, rescue specialists with monitoring equipment detected movement under a concrete slab.

'Rescue team working overhead, can anyone hear me?' one of the men yelled.

'I can hear you!' Stuart called out.

The rescue expert asked if Stuart had any injuries and he shouted back, 'No, but my feet are bloody cold!'

It was another eleven hours before Stuart was carried out of the debris. A close-up image of his dazed face, eyes adjusting to the light, hair caked with plaster dust, is one of the most famous news photographs in Australian history.

The rescue of Stuart Diver is imprinted on the national consciousness in almost the same way as Australia winning the America's Cup in 1983 or Cathy Freeman winning a gold medal at the Sydney Olympics in 2000. It was as if the whole nation was collectively holding its breath and then exhaled as one when he was pulled out. An exhilarating moment of human triumph against impossible odds, and millions of Australians shared it through their television sets. Children sent their teddy bears to Stuart in hospital, grandmothers knitted socks for his cold feet, and the letters he received numbered in the thousands. He couldn't go anywhere without somebody slapping him on the back to say, 'Good on you.'

'Everyone who's ever come up to me has always had great, positive things to say,' Stuart tells me. 'But that also makes it harder to deal with the pain and the anguish and grieving.'

'To lose not only my wife, but the sixteen other people I knew, it was a massive tragedy. That was a lot of grieving to do. In everything I did after, I had this feeling that anything I did was going to affect not just my family but their families as well – if I was on TV and bringing up the memories, all that stuff. So that's a huge amount of pressure for a 27-year-old.'

The media interest was biblical in its intensity. Like James Scott, Stuart Diver was one person at the centre of a gigantic story. Everybody clamoured for the first interview, and as did the Scott family, the Divers hired celebrity agent Harry M. Miller to take charge. Unlike James, though, Stuart was pleased with how it worked out.

'Harry treated me like a son. He was the most ruthless nego-tiator in the history of the world but he protected us from absolutely everything. He just wanted to maintain the integrity of the "Stuart Diver brand". If you look at me now, twenty years on, unless I haven't read it, there's not been a negative article written about me. I've put all that down to having Harry. I have recommended a professional media manager to people going through tragedy on multiple occasions. It's the only way to go.'

But even with a skilled agent, a friendly media and a supportive public, Stuart was still damaged by the process.

'The attention of the media was very much in that positive vein but then I also made a conscious choice to go overtly over the top and make it even more positive, because I wanted to portray that image that you can get through anything; the community of Thredbo will survive, I'll go on, it'll all be good. I didn't want to be the *60 Minutes* clown, sitting there bawling my eyes out on TV. I cried before the interviews or after. I wanted to portray this confident, positive "you can get through anything in your life" idea. But that was hugely detrimental to me in the long-term.'

'Why was that?'

'Firstly, some people looked at me and thought, Wow, he's cold and callous and hard. But two, it also made it harder to deal with the pain and the grief. I think it took me a long time to really, truly grieve Sally's death, because of that.'

I can't fathom the way Stuart lost Sally. It feels like the kind of fever nightmare from which you wake sweaty with terror; the type that makes you turn on the light and climb out of bed, get a glass of water and reassure yourself that it didn't actually happen. It's hard to think that an equivalent horror really did happen to the person sitting opposite me.

When I ask Stuart how he came to terms with losing his wife in that way, he says, 'You have to look at it and say, I've only got two choices. One is to sit there and to be miserable, which you're allowed to do. I'm allowed to feel sorry for myself, some shit things have happened. I do that. But I'm not allowed to do that all the time. Then you'll just go insane. If you look at Sally dying in that landslide, at the end of the day, there's nothing I could have done to save her. And you look at that circumstance and think, What did I do right in those seconds when the building was coming down? I tried to get out myself, but obviously that wasn't going to happen. Then I tried to do what I could to save her life. In the most stressful situation of my life, I tried to look after myself – human instinct – and then I tried to stop her from drowning. If you look at that, it's pretty tragic. But it's also not, because one of my fundamental beliefs is that you care for your fellow human beings. It's looking after each other. So in the most stressful part of my life, I did that.'

Stuart has had years of extensive professional counselling to retrain his brain so that he can replace the thought of how helpless he was when Sally died with the truth that he tried everything he could to save her, showing how much he cared. He has learned to substitute memories of Sally's last moments with thoughts of wonderful times from their lives together – a great trip, a fun birthday, some other special occasion. In the corner of his living room is a bicycle that he rides every night, and he likens keeping his mental health on track to keeping physically fit. It's hard. It requires practice and it takes discipline.

Stuart calls the replacement of sad and negative thoughts with positive ones 'locking away memories'. Having that tool meant that when his second wife was diagnosed with cancer and they knew she was going to die, he already had some ideas about how to ready himself. He hadn't had the chance to prepare for losing Sally, but he drew on the recovery work he did after her death to help him brace for life without Rosanna. He and Rosanna knew that she was terminally ill for a long time, and they worked together to start the grieving process, including locking away memories.

'There's millions of ways of doing it,' he says of this process, 'but the best photographs are a great way. There are little things, like if you go out and have a great dinner one night, you keep the cork. So you have a bottle of Grange, you keep the cork. You leave the cork sitting on the mantelpiece. Then every time you look at that cork, rather than thinking how the person's not here, how devastating it is that the person died, it instantly brings out what an unbelievable dinner that was or what an amazing time we had.

'You're doing all the stuff,' he goes on, 'so that the moment she actually dies, you've pretty well grieved, it's done. People are going to say that's hardcore, like that sounds very cut and dried and clinical. But for me, it was unbelievable. We did the same with Alessia. Alessia was only four, but the whole time leading into when Rosanna died was all about this locking away of these memories, talking about love, talking about families always looking after each other, talking about how everyone always lives in your heart.'

Stuart points to a huge chest in the centre of the living room. 'This whole chest here, it's full of clothes and presents. Rosanna wrote birthday cards for Alessia until she's eighteen. She put together a whole recipe book of her favourite recipes. It was the hardest thing I ever did, hard for Rosanna too. It's amazing – as humans, even when we've got the opportunity to prepare for someone's death, 95 per cent of people won't do it because it's too hard. Then the person dies and they freak out and it goes bananas. "I wish I'd discussed that with them, I wish I'd done that." It's because it's such a hard thing to do.'

'You can only do that if you let go of all the language around cancer, like "You have to keep fighting,"' I suggest.

'That's right.'

'You have to stop having any level of denial about it.'

'Absolutely. You know, when it ends, when the person in front of you stops breathing and they're dead – I thought I'd prepared a huge amount, but nothing prepares you for that. You look at them and you think it's going to fuck up your brain for a long time. But with Rosanna, it didn't. Even walking out of that hospital room an hour later, I felt this amazing sense of calmness, purely because she was no longer in pain. She was no longer suffering. I had Alessia with me and I had this feeling that every-thing was going to be okay. You know,' he says, 'I can compare because I've lost two wives in very different circumstances. One I could prepare for and one I was totally unprepared for. There's only one way to do it, if you can, and that's the way I did it with Rosanna.'

'If I had said to you when you were twenty-five, "Here's what's going to happen to you over the next twenty years," would you have thought you'd have the resilience?' I ask.

'Not at all, I would have had a heart attack. I would have gone, There's absolutely no way, and I definitely wouldn't have thought I'd come out of it at the end like I am, happy, enjoying life,' Stuart says. 'I've always said it's much easier to *be* me than to be someone *observing* me, wondering how I got through stuff. I just did. It just happened.'

When I first contemplated approaching Stuart for this book, I was reluctant because I knew he had endured twenty years of unsought fame and that he had recently lost Rosanna. I made contact through a mutual friend and left it to Stuart to email me if he was interested. When he got in touch and we talked, he reassured me that there was nothing I could ask him that would cause him any further grief, that he had done a huge amount of work to come to terms with what had happened to him.

Sitting across from Stuart in person, I can see that this is true. I might almost think that he is *too* together, except that some of his answers reveal real vulnerability, like his fear that nobody will be able to handle being the third Mrs Diver. He comes back to that a few times, so it clearly weighs on him. I'm surprised at how unguarded he is, because people who've dealt with a lifetime of journalists are often cagey. I'm also struck by his very method-ical and practical way of thinking. I can only assume that he must have always been resilient and emotionally resourceful and that the tragedies have amplified those qualities rather than instilled them. Stuart himself insists that at his core, he is the same person he was before both events.

Even with his reassurance that I should ask whatever I want, there's one question I'm nervous to put. It's about his daughter.

'You know more than anyone that life can deliver horrible blindsides,' I start with trepidation. 'Do you worry, What if something bad happens to Alessia?'

Stuart doesn't seem at all offended or rattled by the question. In hindsight, I guess it's obvious that when a person has faced as much tragedy as he has, he would of course have already contemplated the very worst thing that could ever happen to him.

'I prepare myself for that too. It sounds a bit macabre, but I prepare in my mind for if, say, Alessia drowned in a swimming pool. It would just be devastatingly terrible. But then I do that thing where I look at the six years of her life. I mean, the first four of them she spent every day with Rosanna. That for her was an unbelievable upbringing. She's had three amazing overseas trips. She's been surrounded by love, everyone in Thredbo just loves her. She's had the most amazing life ever. So if it had to happen, I've already set up in my mind, "What an incredible life." We just had the best five weeks ever together in the US. It was amazing. We skied every single day together for five hours. We had our routine of five runs and a hot chocolate. We went to a whole lot of different places. So no matter how tragic it would be for me afterwards, that's what I've locked away.'

'Most people live their lives not really thinking about stuff like this,' I say. 'Most people don't walk down the street every day thinking, I'm vulnerable. We have this sense of invincibility. Do you think your experiences have caused you to reassess your values in life?'

'I never had to look at my values or my belief system before the landslide. When I saw my psychologist we worked out, I think,

I had something like thirteen or sixteen fundamental beliefs. Like one of them is care for people. You can ask my family and good friends who knew me before: I'm the same person. I think that really came from having a great upbringing from my mum and dad, just a good moral compass.'

'You've had two very big whacks in your life and I'm sure plenty of small ones too. Do you think resilience is a finite pool?'

'No, I think you bounce back,' Stuart says. 'I feel more resilient than I ever have.'

And then, just as I'm starting to wonder again if I'm getting anywhere near the real Stuart Diver – because how can anyone be this together after what he's been through – his vulnerability surfaces once more and he says, 'The bit that worries me emotionally, if you look at my life, is how much more love do I have to give? Is that a finite resource?' Stuart sounds so weary when he says this that I'm in fear of choking up. I see that not even somebody as resilient as he is immune from fear and doubt.

'Sally was different,' he continues, 'but with Rosanna, looking after her, caring for her, that outpouring of emotion every single day of your life, it's so traumatic and big. I did think maybe I wouldn't have another relationship because maybe I'm done. But in the last eighteen months, I've more been thinking maybe I've got that back to front. There are rewards you get from that emotional involvement with someone going through that. And also from my emotional involvement now with Alessia, the love we have for each other. So I actually think the pool, the reserves are endless.'

As if on cue, I hear the front door open and the most adorable six-year-old girl with wavy brown hair comes bounding in with her cousin. It's Alessia, back to hang out with her dad. I've brought her a couple of colourful hair clips and when I hand them over she slides them into her fringe and dashes off for a look in the mirror. She must be pleased because, without a word, she comes back and throws her arms around my waist in a tight hug and then skips off again. Stuart has had to face a lot of death in his years but Alessia is such a powerful life force that I can see how much she must help him keep putting one foot in front of the other. Besides his daughter, Stuart has a lot of reasons to enjoy life in fact: his friends, his job as Resort Operations Manager at Thredbo, his love of skiing and the outdoors. Life has delivered some gigantic blows but it has also delivered some beautiful gifts.

Stuart is acutely aware of this, and just before I close my notebook he displays some of the glass-half-full, resilient thinking that has kept him going. 'My whole life has been unbelievable experiences, whether they've resulted in something fantastic or something tragic. I've led the most amazing life ever.'

I have a three-hour drive ahead of me after I leave Stuart and Alessia, through scrubby bush and rolling farmland, back to Canberra and my flight home. I turn the radio off and drive in silence, thinking about Stuart. What an incredible person he is, to go through those devastating events and not become bitter or fearful or crazy. I marvel at the strength and discipline it must have taken to adapt to what life has handed him. Imagine the day he learned he was going to be widowed a second time and would have to raise his little girl alone. And look, I'm not going to lie, my thoughts aren't all deep and worthy – I also start mentally running through a list of my single girlfriends, wondering which of them I could set up with Stuart. I'm pretty sure that contrary to his fear that nobody could handle being the third Mrs Diver, I could hustle together a quality shortlist.

Having covered many tragedies as a journalist, I know that not everybody manages like Stuart Diver. There's such wide variation in the way people take life's left hooks. Some find sustenance deep in reserves they never knew they had. Others turn their pain outwards and use it to campaign for change, so that nobody else has to endure the same thing. I think of Rosie Batty, whose son Luke was murdered by his father, and her extraordinary single-mindedness in forcing Australians to confront domestic violence.

But not all of us can be a hero or an inspiration, and nor should that be the expectation. You'd entirely understand if Walter or Rosie or Stuart were never able to leave the house again. Could you or I carry on if we were in their place? I've covered stories where people have been so confounded by what's happened to them that they've become stuck. The traumatised brain revs like a car in neutral, expending its energy by frantically spinning its engine higher and higher while it goes nowhere.

Of all the tragedies I've covered, one that has stayed with me for many years is the story of Judy Kovco. Her son, Private Jake Kovco, was killed in the Iraq War in 2006, the first Australian casualty. Many Australians would remember his name because of an appalling mix-up with his body after his death. The military accidentally left Kovco's casket behind in a chaotic Kuwaiti morgue, instead flying home the casket of a Bosnian military contractor, draped with an Australian flag. Somehow, the mistake was realised en route. The Australian Minister for Defence at the time, Brendan Nelson, informed the Kovco family as they waited at the airport for the plane to arrive. It was an unforgivable error, one that caused a suffering family immense further pain.

The Kovco case was also marked by much military secrecy and obfuscation, which created the perception of a cover-up. Ultimately, two separate inquiries – one inside and one outside the military – found there was nothing sinister at work, and that Jake Kovco had accidentally killed himself while skylarking with his own gun in his barracks.

Jake was an only child and his mother, Judy, was shattered. Because of the way her grief played out, she could not accept any explanation that had Jake himself at fault. Judy was the one who pushed for the second, independent coronial inquiry after she dismissed the military investigation's findings. She desperately wanted an outcome that didn't blame her own son. Was it a murder? An accident that was being hushed up to protect other soldiers?

Watching Judy testify at the second inquest was an unsettling experience for everybody there. She looked perfectly together, with her neatly made-up face, coiffed blond hair and calm voice, but something was amiss. She seemed oddly absent, as if she had roused herself only momentarily from a bed of grief. She grimaced strangely and attempted jokes that fell flat. She stared into the distance with a half-smile on her face, as though she and her son were having a private conversation in her head.

'I still feel today that I made perfection,' Judy declared to the courtroom at one point.

There was an awkward pause.

'By perfection, you are referring to your son?' a lawyer asked.

'Of course,' she replied, as if puzzled that this wasn't entirely obvious to all present. 'Jake was perfect.'

The way she said it, it wasn't simply a mother's hyperbole; she appeared to believe it was objectively true. Judy made other jarring pronouncements too, such as that she and her son had not a single secret between them. On the stand, she never burst into tears or lost control, yet the impression she gave was of a bird trapped inside a house, frantically flying in circles, smashing into the windows trying to escape. When she stepped down, every person in that courtroom would have been in no doubt as to how thoroughly her son's death and the bungled return of his body had annihilated his mother. My heart ached for her.

When any person suffers a traumatic blindside, they will usually fall apart initially but eventually – and incredibly – the majority adapt to their new normal. Just how long they stay in the first phase and how well they adapt during the second differs enormously. Why do some people seem to remain fractured for a long time while others seem to fairly rapidly return to basic func-tioning? What are the factors that make adaptation more likely?

On arriving home from Thredbo, I once again turn to psy-chological research. It seems to me that the things that influence how well we adjust to a game-changer can be divided into three groups: the nature of the event itself; our genetics; and our internal beliefs about the way the world works, formed largely through our personal history.

That the nature of the event itself dictates how well a person recovers seems self-evident. Stuart Diver's experiences prove that point – as he explained, watching his first wife die in front of him was more traumatic than the death of his second wife, for which he had time to prepare. Many events in life are difficult to process, but some – such as the death of a child or witnessing the violent death of a loved one – are particularly confronting, as is an event in which a person's own life is seriously and suddenly threatened.

Beyond the event itself, our biology and the character traits we inherit from our parents account for about 40 to 50 per cent of how well or otherwise we adapt to adversity. This is no doubt why Stuart commented, 'You can ask my family and good friends who knew me before: I'm the same person.' He's probably right. The fact that he was already resilient, determined and positive would have helped him enormously in coming to terms with his tragedies.

The personality traits associated with recovery include optimism, extroversion, hardiness and a healthy ego. Optimists are more likely, for example, to be able to make meaning of an awful event by concentrating on the good that may come from it, such as Walter Mikac taking comfort in the Alannah & Madeline Foundation. Being optimistic is linked with positive outcomes in numerous studies of affliction, including cancer, heart disease, rheumatic disorders and HIV. The research is so overwhelming that it perhaps explains why we seem to live under the tiresome tyranny of 'positive thinking', as if optimism itself is a miracle cure and not just a coping tool. Telling people they need to 'think positive' if they're not so inclined is potentially harmful, as it can lead to repression or feelings of failure.

One influential theory about adaptation is that we are all born with a fixed level of emotional equilibrium and happiness called a set point. It's kind of like an internal spirit level. Good or bad fortune makes it fluctuate in the short term but then it returns to its original level.

In a famous 1978 study on this matter, researchers compared three groups of people: a control group, a group of lotto winners, and a group of people who had recently suffered devastating spinal injuries. Short-term, winning lotto was definitely a big boost and losing mobility was obviously terrible. But after a year, things had changed. The lotto winners were not significantly happier than the control group. The spinal-cord injury individuals were less happy than both the control group and the lotto winners, but nowhere near as unhappy as they had been straight after their accidents. In 2013, a similar study concluded. It had used different groups of people and looked at them not one year after their original injury, but twenty years later. Over the two decades, all three groups had adapted to their changed circumstances and returned to their original set points.

Since that 1978 study, psychologists have raised questions about whether our equilibrium is really so fixed. A German study monitored 40,000 people for twenty-one years and a British one followed 27,000 people for fourteen years. Charting huge groups of people for such a long time allowed the researchers to scrutinise the impact of all sorts of major life events – divorce, death of loved ones, unemployment, loss of children, and the onset of disabilities. Some people did find their set points enhanced or depressed permanently. It's an area that's ripe for future research.

Stuart Diver said another thing during our interview that, along with his personality, is key to understanding the process of adaptation. He told me that with the help of a therapist he worked out that before the landslide, he held 'thirteen or sixteen fundamental beliefs' – core assumptions about how the world operates. All of us, whether consciously or unconsciously, hold these ingrained beliefs, called schemas. They differ for each of us. They form in our earliest years, through our personal experiences and what adults teach us. A devastating event smashes a person's schemas, causing a kind of mental car crash. Sometimes schemas are pieced back together again and sometimes they are destroyed and replaced by something else.

One person holds many different schemas, covering beliefs about justice, control, predictability, spirituality and self-esteem. Juliet Darling and I rattled through a few at the end of our conversation: things work out for the best, hard work pays off, what doesn't kill you makes you stronger. The most common schemas can be classified into three categories. The first is about the benevolence of the world, notions like 'if you're a good person, good things will come' or 'love will ultimately triumph over hate'. The second covers how the external world works, such as 'people get what's coming to them' or 'your fate is set from birth'. The third is about self-esteem, and might include such ideas as 'I must be a bad person because bad things always happen to me' or 'I've worked hard, so I will achieve my dreams'.

Schemas, whether you're aware of yours or not, powerfully influence your thoughts, actions and behaviour. They're the filter through which you interpret other people's behaviour and they help you decide how to act with friends and strangers. They also help you anticipate and plan for the future, and they even govern what you notice and what you remember when new information comes along. We all pay more attention to things that reinforce our schemas and downplay or negate incoming data that conflicts with them – something known as confirmation bias.

Confirmation bias helps us remain emotionally and mentally stable. As we've seen, humans are predisposed to desire cause and effect. We need explanations for why things happen so that our brains can move on to thinking about something else. The more an incident fits into our existing schemas, the easier it is for the brain to file it away. A sudden, life-changing event is mentally and emotionally destructive because it shatters schemas and stops the brain from knowing how to understand or interpret the world – How could something so awful happen to my child? What did I do to deserve this? I'm a good person!

When schemas are up-ended, the human brain responds in one of three ways. It can go into denial, shutting down, repressing reaction and refusing to process what has happened. Denial can actually be a useful short-term coping mechanism, because it's protective. Or the brain can assimilate, finding a way to integrate what happened into schemas, as Stuart did when he learned to think about his final moments with Sally as evidence that he was somebody who cared about other people, even under the greatest possible stress. The third way is accommodation. This is when a person fundamentally changes a core belief about how the world works. Juliet no longer believing that things will work out for the best if you're a good person is an example of accommodation. The more successfully a person is able to respond in the second or third of these ways, the better they will be able to adapt to a blindside and move forward.

An attempt to make a tragedy fit with our schemas is one of the reasons we almost always ask, 'Why me?' after something awful happens to us. And in fact this is a profoundly important question, because it's the first step in helping the brain process the event. There are literally dozens of studies cataloguing how many people ask themselves this after a traumatic incident – it's almost universal – and what impact the exploration of that question has on recovery.

One of the most influential of these studies involved twenty-nine full-time patients at the Rehabilitation Institute of Chicago. Aged from sixteen to thirty-five, all had become paraplegics or quadriplegics in serious accidents, victims of the type of random calamity that could befall any of us. Among the group were eleven car crashes, six diving accidents and four shootings, along with a private-plane crash, a motorcycle accident, a hang-gliding accident, a tumble down a flight of stairs, a dive into a haystack, and a high school football tackle. There was also a victim of a falling beam in a farm building, and another of a falling piece of machinery. Each case was in itself a rich story of luck, fate, chance, and sliding doors.

The researchers interviewed each patient, along with their doctors and carers, to get a sense of how well or otherwise they were coping with the aftermath of their accident. Every single patient had spontaneously asked themselves, 'Why me?' as soon as they were able. Their answers fell into six categories: pre-determination, probability, chance, God, deservedness, and re-evaluation of the event as a positive. The most popular answer was that God had a reason, and the person had to trust in that reason whether or not it made sense to them (much like Louisa Hope and Michael Spence). Putting the tragedy down to chance was also a very common explanation, along the lines of 'It was just a freak accident that could have happened to anybody.'

There's a fascinating correlation between the answers to 'Why me?' and the ability to cope. Those people coping best answered in a way that indicated they believed they couldn't have avoided the accident, or that ultimately it was their own fault, not somebody else's. For example, one patient who was managing well said, 'It was bound to happen eventually . . . I've been driving around fifteen years . . . you know that eventually, somewhere, there's a fatal accident around.' If the activity was something the person chose to do freely and regularly, they were inclined to see the accident as something that could have happened to anyone and that they were simply unfortunate.

The people who coped worst were those injured doing something they wouldn't normally do (for example, they had accepted a lift in a car when they usually travelled another way), because they saw the accident as something they could have avoided and they found it hard to stop ruminating on the 'if only' scenario. The brain couldn't file the event away. Poor coping also correlated with blaming somebody else for what had happened. Among the worst copers was the sole person who had not been able to come up with any answer at all to the 'Why me?' question. It seems that almost any explanation, even one as odd as 'The devil got into God that night and made God do something wrong' (another patient's offering) is better as a coping mechanism than no explanation at all. Any story that allows the brain to maintain the illusion that there's an underlying order and meaning to our existence helps with recovery.

When the brain keeps ruminating on an awful event (keeping it in what psychologists call the active memory), it torments a person with intrusive, recurrent thoughts. Sometimes this is because the gap between what happened and a person's schemas is too difficult to bridge. Other times, the brain can't easily construct new schemas. It's what causes a person to have difficulty moving on, or 'finding closure' as the annoying term has it. As I've mentioned, short-term, this mental train wreck happens to almost everyone who's shattered by grief or a terrible event, and most people do adapt. But failure to adapt is not uncommon, and it causes predictably dysfunctional behaviour – people can begin to obsess over conspiracy theories, they may ascribe blame or intent where there is none, and they sometimes write endlessly to authorities or demand inquiries.

In legal circles, these people are known as querulous complainants. They pop up so regularly that *The Australasian Coroner's*

Manual includes a section on how to compassionately manage them. It notes that 'they are relentlessly driven by a pursuit of justice . . . [Their] complaints cascade in type and target over the years and secondarily devastate their own lives.' Families can split and people can lose jobs and friends because their brains become so stuck on the unfairness or inexplicability of what has happened.

Skimming through the *Coroner's Manual* makes me realise something. Nearly every case I've looked at so far in this book wound up before a coroner. There were inquests into the Lindt Café siege, the Port Arthur massacre, the Toowoomba floods, the deaths of Nick and Chloe Waterlow, the Thredbo landslide, and the case of Private Kovco. I wonder if a coroner, a person whose job immerses them in unexpected tragedy every day, might be able to explain a little more about how people react when life blindsides them.

I need to find the name of the coroner who sat on the bench when I slipped into the public gallery every day to report on the Kovco inquest. She had a kindly way about her, that's all I remember.

I keep my notebooks and papers from the two Kovco inquiries in a large maroon cardboard box on the top shelf of my linen cupboard. Taking it down and spreading the pages on the floor of my study, I see that the coroner in the case was Mary Jerram. I also see that, time and again, I've remarked on her compassion in my notes. She had such an encouraging and sympathetic way about her, always putting people at ease. There's even a letter that I wrote to her but never posted. 'Dear Magistrate Jerram,' it reads, '. . . I thought many times during the hearings that if ever I was in the unfortunate situation of having to appear at such an inquest, I would hope to be in front of somebody as thoughtful and decent as you.'

'That's nice to hear,' says Mary Jerram when I go to visit her, almost ten years after tucking that letter into a notebook and forgetting about it. In a stroke of good luck for me, Mary, who retired in 2013, is back for a stint as Acting New South Wales Coroner, and the court where she works every day is just a ten-minute walk from where I live. She's been asked to fill in while her successor, Michael Barnes, presides over the lengthy Lindt Café inquest. The interruption to her retirement was meant to last for only a few weeks but it's turned into months.

Mary is in her late sixties and has short brown hair. She wears a black turtleneck with a jacket over the top and a chunky brown and orange necklace with yellow resin earrings. Her glasses have black and red frames and she gestures with them in her right hand as we talk. She has sparkly eyes and a bright, energetic manner, and although there's a gigantic wooden desk in her office, she ushers me to a couple of comfortable armchairs facing each other so we can sit and chat more informally.

If you're a fan of Patricia Cornwell's Kay Scarpetta novels, or you watch *NCIS*, you may think a coroner is somebody who heads to crime scenes in the middle of the night, snaps on latex gloves and picks wet leaves off corpses, regularly finding clues that the police miss, such as tiny letters of the alphabet inserted under fingernails. I'm sorry to shatter the illusion, but in Australia that's not what a coroner does. Here, they are not medical examiners or profilers. They don't perform autopsies or do forensic work at crime scenes, although they can observe that if they wish. Australian coroners are lawyers by training, usually former magistrates or judges.

A coroner is basically a fact-finder. Their job is to inquire into sudden, unexpected, unexplained, violent or suspicious deaths. They try to find out how an individual died. Was somebody responsible? Are there wider implications? A coronial inquest is not a trial, although it can recommend that people be charged, and unlike a trial, an inquest doesn't have to prove something 'beyond reasonable doubt'. The standard is 'on the balance of probabilities'. To get as close as possible to the truth of how some-body's life ended, the coroner will turn over every possible rock and burrow down every last hole, even if it sometimes means that embarrassing facts come to light or privacy is breached. All sorts of different people help the coroner in this detective work: police, lawyers, psychologists, doctors, pathologists, and even experts in fields such as geology or ballistics.

Societies have coroners for two important reasons. One is to ensure accurate death certificates and records. We need to know what kills people because, as I've mentioned, it informs govern-ment policy. The second reason is to assist the peace of mind of the living by improving the safety and quality of life. Events such as the sinking of a ferry or the collapse of a bridge require a reassurance to the public that similar tragedies will be avoided in future. If governments or other people have been negligent, a coroner will demand accountability for those directly affected and for the broader public. Allowing a coroner that power is a way for governments to signal to their citizens that they value individual lives.

A coroner's work is frequently fascinating, because it canvasses unusual and rare deaths around which there is a degree of mystery. There's a high overlap with the types of random and cruel deaths that end up on the news.

'Isn't the job depressing?' I ask Mary Jerram.

'We always get asked here if it's depressing,' she says. 'Actually it's not depressing, it's too interesting.'

Mary makes me laugh by revealing that I'm asking the wrong question. Forget about depression, anxiety is the problem.

'My husband is now seventy-three, so he coughs and I think, Oh shit, he has cancer,' says Mary. 'Or he's in the garden for much longer than I expected and I think, I'd better have a look.'

People going to the bathroom and never returning have also appeared often enough in cases before Mary for her to get a niggle when somebody disappears from the dining table for a little too long. And as for police reports on crime scenes, you'll never leave your house in the same state again once you've read a few of those.

'They always say things like "The house was quite tidy but there was an unwashed cup in the sink." Every time I leave the house now, I think, What have I left unwashed today?' She laughs.

Mary's first career was high school teaching but she figured out fairly quickly that it wasn't for her, and so while her children were small she started studying law, staying up late and doing her coursework while they were in bed. After finishing her degree, she worked in industrial law and then in legal aid, and by the 1990s she was a full-time magistrate, ultimately rising to the role of New South Wales Deputy Chief Magistrate. In 2007, she was appointed State Coroner. The high-profile inquest into Jake Kovco's death was the first major case she heard in that role and she remembers it well.

'I think poor Mrs Kovco was so extreme when giving her evidence about her adoration of Jake that perhaps she became less credible,' she recalls. 'I think everyone felt for her grief, but she couldn't accept or overcome the facts which the jury obviously accepted – that he was fooling around with his gun that evening.'

'Did you feel that the inquest actually found out the truth of what happened?' I ask.

'I really did. There were eight weeks of evidence before a six-person jury and they were all dedicated and attentive the whole time. There was no other possible finding.'

Another of the things that has stayed with me about the Kovco case is the gap between the court's view of the outcome and the mother's view. The court believed that justice had been served. Judy Kovco did not. In my experience, this disconnect between justice as lawyers see it and justice as the public sees it is not uncommon. Once you or somebody you love is a victim, the presumption of innocence seems a bit less straightforward. Sitting in a hearing, it can sometimes feel like everything is biased towards the accused. Somebody who appears guilty gets off due to a lack of evidence or a technicality. To non-lawyers, some legal rules can be maddening, such as the fact that a person's prior convictions are inadmissible. The law says that just because somebody has committed violent acts in the past, for example, doesn't mean they're guilty of doing so now. But to the non-lawyer, common sense would dictate that if a person has a long track record of violent offences, they're probably more likely to be guilty. If I were on a jury I would want that information about prior convictions, but I wouldn't be allowed to have it.

Sentencing is a particularly sore point, and a regular source of outrage on talkback radio or among politicians. Sometimes we can't understand why the punishment doesn't fit the crime. While many people do leave court feeling satisfied with the process, others can't shake the feeling that they didn't receive justice.

'Why do you think there's this disconnect?' I ask Mary Jerram.

'I think that when you're talking about major things like murder and rape, there probably never is any justice. Of course, in a primitive society, it would be that you'd be allowed to go and thrust the culprit with a spear. Do we really want that sort of society?' she asks. 'I think some people do, or think they would. You hear often the next of kin after a trial where there's been a murder, particularly, saying, "Our family's wrecked, and he's going to be out in twenty years and that's not justice." But what do they really mean? Do they think that person should have gone to the chair?'

'I do think a lot of people feel that way,' I say. 'If it were my child, I would feel that way.'

'But is it justice or vengeance?' Mary asks. 'I think it is the latter that is often voiced by distressed people.'

'Isn't it a problem that there's this gap between what the public thinks of as justice and what lawyers think of as justice?' I put to her.

'Unfortunately, radio shock jocks and some newspapers don't help in presenting facts truthfully, so there's a lot of misunder-standing about the legal system. I think often people who think there hasn't been justice are often not very aware of all the facts. There are many people who do believe that, generally, our system is as good as it can be.'

When Mary Jerram was hearing the Kovco matter, Judy Kovco's shattered demeanour was sadly familiar, as Mary herself had been blindsided by her own family tragedy just weeks before.

'The first few months I was here, I had this brilliant niece who was just finishing her PhD in seismic engineering in Grenoble – she'd done it in French,' Mary says.

Her name was Jane Jerram and she was twenty-five.

'She and her boyfriend and two other international students, early summer, decided to go to Mont Blanc because they'd all just finished. And they were hit by a terrible and unexpected storm and they all died. The worst part was that her boyfriend, who knew the most about mountaineering, died first and the others didn't know how to work the emergency equipment. But they did have mobiles. Calls were recorded as they died one by one. I've never listened to those but I think my brother did.'

Mary's brother and sister-in-law, who were living in New Zealand, were so stricken with grief that they lost their senses for a time.

'The interesting thing about general grief,' Mary says, 'is that my brother was a vet and his wife was a science teacher of many years and they both for a short while became quite irrational. They blamed the French police for not getting there fast enough. They blamed the boyfriend. But they weren't really like that normally; they're sensible, educated.'

'Could they see they were being irrational?' I ask.

'I don't think so, but they did stop it once she'd been buried and there had been a memorial service, which took a month or two. I don't know if they'll ever get over it. My husband went with Pete, my brother, to take her ashes up onto the slopes behind Grenoble and he said Pete just wept the whole time.'

'Did your professional experience give you any particular skills to cope with what occurred in your own family?' I ask.

'Yeah, it probably did. I do remember sitting there' – she points to the large wooden desk that dominates the room – 'and weeping badly the first day or two. It was more the other way around, it helped me to understand families better after that.'

On the very day I'm here at the coroner's court with Mary, staff at the morgue are dealing with an Iraqi family in the grip of terrible irrationality following the death of their eighteen-year-old daughter.

'The family won't agree to a post-mortem, but she's got to have one because there's no known cause of death, it was very sudden. But they truly think she's going to rise again today, which is the seventh day,' Mary tells me.

This is a big problem, because the more time that elapses before an autopsy, the further the body decays, and the harder it is to discover the cause of death. The morgue staff are beside themselves because they can't delay a moment longer, yet the family can't be persuaded.

(I email Mary Jerram a few days later to ask what happened and she replies that the family somehow came around to accepting they had to say goodbye and allow the autopsy. Their daughter's death was found to be the result of a serious cardiac problem.)

A coroner is meant to be impartial and dispassionate, and yet sometimes that's very difficult. One of the cases that most affected Mary in her years as coroner was that of Raymond Cho, a sixteen-year-old schoolboy who died of anaphylactic shock after eating a walnut biscuit in his school playground. The boy's friend had baked the biscuit in cooking class. Raymond knew that he had a nut allergy and he also knew that the biscuit had walnuts in it, and yet he took a bite. Nobody could ever figure out why. One student gave evidence that Raymond thought it would probably be okay because the nuts weren't peanuts. The student who shared the biscuit had to testify, as did the teachers who administered first aid. The family was asked at the end of the inquest if they would like to say anything.

'And the older sister,' Mary recalls, 'who must have been about fifteen, a very articulate girl, stood up and read this beautiful thing about him and how lovely he was. But then she said, "We used to be a happy family. And now I hear my mother crying all night long through the wall and her hair is coming out." And it was. I looked. Her mother had this great bald patch. Then the father almost threw himself to the floor and wept. And I thought,

I've got to sit here and try and look professional. I looked around the court and almost every single person in the courtroom had tears rolling down their cheeks. In the end, I knew I had to wipe my eyes. But I don't think it necessarily helps people for you to collapse.'

Mary, too, hates the word 'closure'. When you meet people like the Cho family, or Judy Kovco, you know there is never closure. The word is an insult. The best they can hope for is to learn to manage and adapt, and perhaps, over time, to once again wake up to a day on which the scales will tip more towards joy than pain.

Six

Out of the Ashes

I'm spending five days alone in a flat at the beach, about an hour and a half south of Sydney. From my seat at the old wooden dining table, I can see the ocean through the window. The cloudless sky is cornflower blue and the sea glints as if a diamond merchant has spread his wares on it. A flock of surfers perches out past the breakers, waiting for the best waves on which to soar back in. On the sand, a couple of dogs chase each other back and forth, barking and frolicking in the water. A mother holds the hands of two children, their chubby bodies shielded from the sun by bucket hats and rashies. They stand at the edge of the water and when the foam surges forward and nibbles at their toes, the little one squeals and bounces in delight.

I love to look at the ocean and listen to its roar but I never go in very far. The powerful push and pull makes me uneasy and the feeling of the sand sucking away beneath my feet unsettles me. I don't like what I can't see under the waves. In John Irving's novel *The World According to Garp*, Garp's son, Walt, mishears the family discussing the undertow at the beach and comes to believe it's called the Under Toad. He imagines a foul beast lurking under the waves, waiting to drag unsuspecting swimmers out. That's how I feel too. I believe in the Under Toad.

Perhaps my desire to stand back and observe from a distance rather than swim into the depths partly explains why I'm a journalist. Watching and reporting feels safer than participating. Unfortunately, that's not how life works; you can find yourself out at sea whether you're comfortable there or not. It is a collective delusion, as Louisa Hope pointed out, to imagine that the ground is firm under our feet or that the water around us will remain warm and calm. The weather can turn in an instant and there's nothing you or I can do about it.

These thoughts, and what I've heard from Stuart and the others, make me wonder again about how people cope after life suddenly changes. Could there be even more to the aftermath of a blindside than adaptation and re-evaluation? What if it actually changes you for the better in the long term? Can a survivor go beyond mere adjustment to tangible positive change? Or is that a lie we tell ourselves so we don't have to confront the thought that our suffering may be in vain?

Two of the men out past the breakers have found the perfect wave and are riding it all the way into the shallows. A third glides sideways inside its barrel, the foam curling over his head as he races to stay ahead of it. Probably none of them gives a moment's thought to the type of dark questions I'm pondering as I look on. Watching their graceful surfing causes me to think about another perfect day at the beach, just like this one, and a young man very much like them.

No matter how miserable the weather or how cosy their bed, when the alarm went off at 5 am every Friday morning, there was nothing Hannah Richell could say to dissuade her husband Matt from going for his weekly pre-dawn surf at Freshwater, in Sydney's northern suburbs.

'It's raining, it's cold!' Hannah would sometimes mumble. 'What are you doing? Stay in bed!'

But off Matt would go. When the couple moved to Australia from the UK in 2005, Matt was determined to learn to surf properly. He bought a sleek surfboard and took lessons for six months. Something in it appealed to his busy mind. Surfing compelled him to slow down, to observe the elements, to patiently wait for his moment. The sound of the waves and the rise and fall of the water was a meditation to him and it was the one place where Matt was free from the pressure of his job as publisher, and later CEO, at Hachette Australia. On the water, there were no demands from authors, no meetings, no need to think about how the digital age was revolutionising the book business. It was just

Matt and the ocean. A Friday morning surf before work wasn't just a hobby for him, it was a necessity.

Matt and Hannah had met in their mid-twenties, when both applied for the same job in London. Matt had been working at Bloomsbury during the Harry Potter juggernaut and was exhausted from the wild ride. Then his mother died and it all became too much. He took a year off to recharge and went backpacking. When he returned, he applied for a job at Pan Macmillan, the firm where Hannah worked. Hannah had her eye on the same position, hoping for a promotion, but Matt beat her to it. She gave him the evil eye for a few weeks when he started, something they laughed about later.

When Hannah was a girl, she had once asked her mother, 'How do you know when you meet the right person?' and her mother had replied with the infuriatingly cryptic 'You just know.' With Matt, Hannah learned that her mother was right: she did just know. They both knew. There were no doubts, no messy break-ups to initiate, no more partying that beckoned. It was as if the universe had orchestrated their best selves to meet at exactly the right time. Matt had a kindly, handsome face with twinkling eyes. Hannah was a writer, a stunning blonde who managed the rare feat of combining elegance with warmth and not haughtiness.

In 2014, life was busy for Matt and Hannah. They had two young children, a boy and a girl, aged three and six. Hannah was writing a book and Matt was frantic at work, organising the company's annual conference as well as training for a half-marathon to raise money for the Sydney Story Factory, a charity that helps disadvantaged children with literacy. He had squeezed in a quick trip to London and also had a slate of writers' festivals to attend all over Australia.

One Wednesday at the start of July that year, Matt and Hannah shared a morning coffee, kissed goodbye and went their separate ways, Hannah to a solitary day of writing and Matt to ponder a new company strategy he would soon present to the Hachette board. He had a plan to meet his friend Adam for a quick lunchtime surf at Bronte in Sydney's eastern suburbs.

Bronte Beach is a picturesque spot, nestled in an alcove at the bottom of a hill, and is popular with families. A wide grassy area dotted with wooden huts faces a small beach about 250 metres long. There's a steep cliff at either end. Regardless of the time of year, there are always people sunbathing on the sand or grass, walking their dogs, or running in a state of partial undress to show off their buff, tanned bodies. On a clear day, the water is a striking azure blue, closer to aqua when you look down upon it from the cliff top.

Surfers seem impervious to most moods of the weather and they can almost always be seen bobbing on the ocean at Bronte, or the next beach along, Tamarama. There's a small rocky outcrop between the two beaches that local surfers refer to as The Twins, for its two large vertical rocks. It's known to be a dangerous spot, with many rips and sharp rocky ledges under the water. If the swell on either side of The Twins is rough, it can push a surfer towards the cliffs where the waves unload. New waves pound the rocks as old ones draw back into the ocean, making it hard to get out of the malevolent churn.

On this particular day, Matt and Adam met as planned at 1.30 pm on Bronte Beach. Not being cavalier men, they took time to study the conditions from the cliff top and to read the surf report. It looked okay and they decided to tackle a break at the northern end of Bronte, adjacent to The Twins. The surf report predicted waves of 2 to 4 feet, and as the friends paddled out, that's exactly what they found. After they'd been surfing for no more than fifteen minutes, Adam tried to catch a wave and was washed close to The Twins. The chaotic and forceful eddies made it hard for him to escape from the rocky area, and once he was clear he warned Matt to be careful. Around the same time, another surfer near the two men, Leigh Jackson, noticed that the conditions had suddenly become a little rougher.

Soon after, a large set of waves loomed further out in the ocean. An unbroken wave is a moving lump of water over which it is easy to manoeuvre a surfboard. Once it breaks, it unloads all its energy. If the board rider is not on top of the wave as it breaks, the only option, to avoid being pummelled, is to dive underneath it. That can be dangerous if the surfer starts to lose breath or panic and so it's always preferable to paddle over the top if possible. As this new set of waves started to build, Adam paddled as fast as he could to ride over them, aware that he wasn't in the right position to surf. He went over the first wave then duck-dived under the next couple. When he came up, he looked behind him to see how Matt had fared. All he saw was Matt's surfboard briefly pop out of the water, in a way that suggested it was unmanned. Adam started paddling over to check that Matt was okay and he saw his friend upright and treading water, near the rocks.

Adam called out to ask if Matt needed help and Matt gestured in a way that Adam couldn't interpret. Although Matt didn't seem panicked, the turbulent water started to sweep him northward towards Tamarama.

A fisherman high up on the rocks had a clear view of what was happening and he watched as Matt was swept into a gap in the rocks where the water was particularly rough. The fisherman called ooo on his mobile phone. At the same time, a nearby member of the public had also been watching with some concern. He walked into the Bronte Surf Livesaving Club to report that a surfer may be in trouble. There was no lifeguard on duty at Bronte that day and so a call went to Bondi Beach, several kilometres away, and an experienced lifesaver raced to them on a jet ski.

Adam did everything he could to reach Matt. The same surfer who earlier noted the deteriorating conditions, Leigh Jackson, also tried. People started to gather on the beach and the cliff top. One of them later described Matt as 'bobbing like a cork'. A bystander on the cliff pointed to a large rock, trying to help Adam spot Matt's whereabouts.

Leigh finally caught sight of Matt again as he was trying to clamber out of the water at the base of the cliff, but before Matt could get clear, a large wave crashed into him, smashing him against the jagged rock face. One of the onlookers shouted, 'He's gone under!' The water receded, taking Matt with it, away from the rocks, and at last both Adam and Leigh reached him. Matt was floating face down with numerous cuts on his head.

The men struggled to get him to the beach. Other people quickly ran to help but he was unconscious and unresponsive.

Before long an ambulance was on the sand. Matt lay flat on his back on the ocean side of the vehicle as paramedics worked on him. They gave Matt repeated doses of adrenalin and oxygen and applied defibrillator pads. Groups of people were standing well back, on either side of the ambulance, watching in horror. A surfer in a wetsuit – Adam – was holding his forehead with both hands. Two police officers were there, one with a hand on his cheek.

Later that afternoon, Hannah arrived back at their cottage from her day of writing. The babysitter was in the back room with the children and she could hear them chortling and playing. In the living room were two strangers, plainclothes police officers waiting for Hannah's return. One of them was a woman and although she wasn't crying, Hannah could see that she looked very upset and knew instantly that something terrible had happened.

'What is it?' she said.

'I'm very sorry to say your husband's been in a surfing accident,' one of them told her.

Hannah recoiled. 'Is he okay?'

The answer was devastating. Matt, only forty-one years old, was dead on the beach even before the ambulance arrived. Everything Hannah had assumed about their future together, about the order of the universe, died along with him. The police said she needed to call somebody to come and sit with her but she didn't want to. That would make it real.

Almost exactly two years later, I ride my Vespa to visit Hannah in a leafy part of Sydney's inner west (and no, it's not lost on me that riding a motorcycle is a provocative act for somebody writing a book about sudden, life-changing disasters). It is just the type of day on which Matt would have loved to go surfing – there's a nip in the air but in the sun it's crisp and pleasant. The sky looks freshly scrubbed to a gleaming blue. It's exhilarating to weave the scooter through the alleys and laneways to Hannah's cottage.

Hannah is putting the rubbish out when I arrive. She wears ugg boots, jeans and a loose jumper and still manages to look stylish. Inside her house it's cosy and inviting. The kids' art is stuck to the fridge and one of the drawings has a caption that reads 'I love my dad so much.' Matt's handsome, open face smiles warmly from a framed picture. Hannah makes tea and we sit at the kitchen table, sharing some treats she's bought from a local patisserie.

I had written to her about a month before we met, explaining the questions I wanted to address in this book. I asked if she'd be willing to talk about the hard trudge through week after week, month after month, of grief. I wanted to know how it had changed her and whether any good had come of it. She agreed to meet because she felt that nobody had much wanted to hear about the aftermath of Matt's death. When she found herself unexpectedly in the midst of trauma, she had no idea how to navigate the terrain because the subject is almost never discussed.

Hannah distinctly remembers the overwhelming feeling, that afternoon when the police told her that Matt had died, of not wanting to tell anybody.

'I just said, "I don't want anyone to know." It was this extreme feeling of embarrassment. I don't know why I was embarrassed.

It was like, This can't be happening to us, and not wanting it to be real,' she says. Reflecting on it now, it seems crazy to Hannah that her first feeling was embarrassment, but that was how her brain and body reacted to the shock.

Although a person dies in Australia every three minutes and seventeen seconds, Matt's death was the one that captured media attention that day. It happened in a public space and he was a young, good-looking man, well known and respected in his field. Australians are also particularly entranced by news stories of mishaps in the ocean, perhaps because going to the beach is such a quintessentially Australian experience, one with which almost everyone can identify. It jars when a blameless person is struck down enjoying a common, pleasurable activity, and the feeling that 'it could have been me' is very strong.

The police gently pointed out to Hannah that there was no way she'd be able to stop Matt's name from imminently appearing in the media. It wouldn't be good for people to find out that way, they said. It meant that Hannah faced the pressure of having to act quickly when she was in deep shock. It wasn't the fault of the police, or even the media necessarily, it was just the way things were.

So she rang her sister in Melbourne. She also had to ring Matt's father in the UK, a dreadful task and one that still haunts her. It was terribly confronting to have to say out loud that Matt had died and then witness everybody bustle into action.

'I didn't want the house filled with people, because in my head I couldn't believe it had happened,' Hannah says. 'My biggest concern was the kids. I felt this overwhelming need to protect them and somehow make it not as awful as it was for them. That's probably why I didn't tell them until the next morning, because I felt like I wanted them to have one more night where it wasn't real.'

At one point late that afternoon, Hannah asked the police if they were sure it was Matt. He had told her he was going to go to Maroubra, a beach further south. Maybe there'd been a mistake? It was definitely him, the police insisted. Soon afterwards, more police officers arrived with Matt's car.

'They turned over his wallet and his wedding ring. That was quite a moment, to be handed a ziplock bag with his wedding ring and wallet. I was just like, Okay, now that feels real.'

By that time, Adam had already formally identified Matt's body, which meant that Hannah didn't have to go to the morgue if she didn't want to.

The question of whether or not to attend a viewing, as it's called, is something many bereaved people grapple with. Some of us are terrified and don't want to. Others aren't sure. Some people are utterly certain straight away that they must see the body. It's a decision that has to be made fairly quickly, and that means it's made in the fresh grip of shock and trauma. If somebody later regrets their decision, it cannot be undone. They may regret being persuaded to do the opposite of their initial preference, or feel they were given inadequate information about what to expect. There is some research that shows it's psychologically useful to attend a viewing, as it helps the bereaved accept the reality of the loved one's death; this is in line with what Steve Sinn firmly believes from his practical experience.

Hannah was one of those people who instantly knew that she needed to see her husband's body. Matt had to have an autopsy first and so it was almost twenty-four hours before she was permitted to see him. She arrived at the morgue late on Thursday afternoon and a woman around her own age met her in the reception area. Hannah recalls that the woman's presence was extraordinarily reassuring.

'She was the first person I felt understood what was happening. She had this incredibly calm, knowledgeable demeanour, which made me instantly feel a bit safer.'

The woman told Hannah what to expect to see. In great detail, she described how Matt was laid out, what he was wearing, even the colour of the sheet covering him and what the wounds on his face and head looked like. The woman asked Hannah if she had any questions and then said she could go in by herself if she wished, or have somebody accompany her. She could touch Matt, she could take as long as she wanted. Hannah steeled herself and walked inside. The woman stayed with her for a couple of minutes and then left her alone.

'It was a bit scary to see him, but not him. He was like a sort of Madame Tussauds model. He didn't have much hair. He had a very shaved head, so you saw the stitches. I was like, That's not Matt. But it was Matt,' says Hannah softly. 'The detail for me that felt the most personal – because they had washed him and put him in a hospital gown – was when I took hold of his hand, there was sand in his palm still. I felt . . . *It's you.*'

Let me break into Hannah's story here to tell you what it's like to sit across from her and hear this. Over the previous hour, she has told me how she and Matt met, what his interests were, what their life was like, how much they loved each other. Here I am, sitting in the very heart of their old life, at their kitchen table, where they would have spent hours with each other and their children. Hannah is so lovely, sitting here, sharing tea with me, trusting me with these intimate details. Matt's face looks at me from the frame nearby. When Hannah tells me that as she caresses his hand, he is still holding the sand from the beach, it takes every last bit of my willpower to not collapse sobbing. It feels as if everything about their story is contained in those grains of sand: the impermanence of life, the swiftness of change. I want to weep at the injustice of it, the cruelty of the loss. If I'm telling this story matter-of-factly, it's because I'm trained by years of practice as a journalist to do it that way. The truth is, as I'm writing these words, tears are streaming down my face.

Once the first few weeks pass after a death, one of the hardest things is that life keeps relentlessly rolling on. Like the ocean, the tides keep rising and falling, the waves breaking and retreating. Everybody returns to their regular routine and there's an expectation that the bereaved person will start the process of 'recovery'. This is very difficult to do because for a grieving person, the most ordinary activities can take on deep meaning that would never cross anybody else's mind.

Hannah says, 'I remember being in the supermarket and someone bumping into me. It was the first time I'd been to the supermarket since Matt had died, probably only two weeks after. I was walking around with the trolley and you're confronted by all the things you don't need to buy anymore. Matt used to have gluten-free bread, for example. I thought, Well, I don't need to buy that anymore. It's the most mundane detail but it kills you inside. And someone bumped into me and didn't say sorry. I didn't do anything but I just wanted to turn around and go, "You don't know what's happened to me! I'm grieving!" It can be the tiniest thing that wounds you.'

'Was there ever a time, as irrational as it might be, when there was a sense of irritation or feeling of "Where *is* he?"' I ask.

'All the time, all the time. I remember "Where are you?" constantly. It felt like someone had literally just rubbed him out. It's baffling, utterly baffling,' Hannah says.

The reaction among Hannah's friends was mixed. Some had a fix-it mentality and constantly offered solutions as to how Hannah could stop feeling so wretched. Some couldn't handle her grief and backed away. Some had their own problems and had no capacity to take on somebody else's. And others of course were amazing. Many offered practical support, like food or babysitting. A kind few had the emotional intelligence to just sit with her and let her fall apart or be in pain. They didn't try to change it or offer platitudes. They were just there, accompanying, to use Steve Sinn's word. Hannah found that was some of the most valuable support.

'Having had this experience, if a friend was going through the loss of a partner or dealing with cancer or something like that, do you think you'd behave differently?' I ask.

'I would for sure. I wouldn't be so scared to be with them. It is scary being with people who are in extreme pain. The fear is you're going to do something that makes it worse. But I know

now the worst thing you can do is ignore it or pretend it's not happening and not be there for them.' Hannah's reply is very similar to the sentiments Walter Mikac expressed.

A few weeks after Matt's death, Hannah felt so dreadful that she arranged to visit a psychologist, a free service offered by the NSW Department of Forensic Medicine. When she arrived for her first appointment, her counsellor turned out to be the same woman who'd helped her with the viewing of Matt's body.

'I talked to her about everything. From the word go, it was everything from "I don't want to live anymore, I can't do this" to "I can't handle the children. How do I cope with their grief when I'm falling apart inside?" There was "I really miss having sex and I feel this incredible shame about wanting to have sex, my husband's just died!" It felt like there was nothing off limits and there was no judgement from her, ever.'

Hannah was grappling with the same questions that many suddenly bereaved people have.

'I remember saying endlessly, "We were so happy, I just don't understand how this could have happened. He was such a good person. There are so many terrible people out in the world and why Matt?"'

There is sometimes an impression that attending counselling is a passive exercise: you see a psychologist, download your feelings and problems, leave, then do the same the following week. But for it to be beneficial, it must be a very active process. A good counsellor will give you a gentle steer about how to move your thinking in new directions. You have to apply yourself to doing that in between visits if you want to grow and adapt.

Hannah began to try it, actively challenging her assumptions about life and death, trying to make sense of what had happened to her.

'I remember thinking, Why us? Very quickly, I got around to, Why not us? There's nothing special about us. And I think sometimes we can live our lives thinking we're in a special bubble, like the world's revolving around us. I had to face the brutal realisation that living a "good" life and doing things in a certain, careful way did not necessarily afford us any special protection or safety. We are each as vulnerable as the next person on the planet, and that was both a terrifying and enlightening fact.'

Because Matt's death was a public event, it was the subject of a coronial inquest to find out exactly what had happened. Everyone who had been at the beach that day – the other surfers, the lifeguard, the fisherman on the rocks – was summonsed to give evidence. Before the inquest started, Hannah thought she already knew all the details, and yet the process was so forensic that new information emerged, and for that, Hannah was grateful.

'Having a witness, someone who was there, who was the person with Matt when he died, was incredibly comforting and helpful to me,' she says. 'For me to work through everything, that sort of detail was invaluable. If it had been shrouded in mystery and I was left with loads of "How did it happen?" kind of questions, I think it would have been a lot harder.'

The formal finding was that Matt died from 'misadventure' when the surf swept him against the rocks of a sea cliff, inflicting incapacitating head injuries that caused him to drown.

The inquest report specifically noted that Matt was a sensible and careful person who surfed responsibly and was well aware of his limitations. In the words of the coroner, it was a 'wretched' event.

The hearings themselves were very rough on Hannah, who spent most of the time in the public gallery weeping quietly.

'I got very drunk the night after the inquest finished, went and drank margaritas with my sister,' she recalls.

By the time the inquest ended, almost two years had passed since Matt's death. But then a few days later, Hannah noticed that she felt different.

'I felt this lightness settling on me, which was new. It's not closure, because I will live with Matt's death and the pain of it every day and the grief will stay with me. I just felt that I was carrying it differently. It was in a place inside me that was more contained, it wasn't all of me. It wasn't like raw, open grief. It was almost like the scab had grown over. Occasionally you pick at it, or it might come off when you're not expecting it and you start bleeding again.'

Hannah has written, in her own words, 'three overwrought diaries', just to let all the grief out. She has had a lot of counselling and done a lot of reading. Some days are better than others.

'My biggest fear now is that I have to go through this again. What's next? Because I know unless I die next, I'm going to lose someone that I love, and the thought of that pain on top of the pain I already carry from Matt feels terrifying. But what do you do then? Do you stop loving people? Of course not. That's why we're here, to love people and to give of ourselves. So I just try and keep myself as open as possible.'

This reminds me of what Stuart Diver said about realising that there is enough love to carry on, that it's boundless.

'I think of the way we can make space in our hearts to love people – you have one child and you think, I could never love another child the way I love my firstborn. Then you have another child and you're like, Oh, I do love them. It's the same and different, because they're a different person. Somehow your heart can expand to carry love for many people. Maybe it's the same with pain. We can carry so much more than we think we can, whether that is love or pain. The pain is love. It's just the manifestation of the sad side of losing someone, as opposed to them being with you.'

There is something beautiful about sitting and listening to Hannah. What she says is deeply insightful. And although we have spoken about such sad things, the atmosphere in the room isn't sad at all. The room feels full of life. Hannah positively pulses with it. It's very attractive, almost magnetic. It's hard to describe but it is as if she is drawn very sharply. I don't know Hannah, we are not friends, and yet we've had a conversation as intimate and real as any I've had in my life.

'I understand now that happiness isn't some goal that we're working towards,' she says near the end of our talk, 'it's just in the daily living of life.'

'It's that we just had a cup of tea and a nice pastry,' I say.

'Exactly. It's just appreciating the small moments. Sitting with you, having this conversation, is really lovely. So it's finding happiness in the day-to-day.'

Hannah has not drastically changed her life since losing

Matt. She lives in the same home, the one they shared. She is still a writer. Superficially, it looks like the same life except without Matt in it. But look more closely and things are not the same at all. After her intense period of grief, Hannah did not return to being the Hannah who was with Matt. That person is gone forever.

'I'm so changed. I'm so different. I feel like I've sort of had a layer of skin removed. I'm still me, I still hold the same values. But I'm able to live my life now in a very different way. I just find peace and beauty in the smallest moments now,' she says. 'I find myself feeling less afraid of life, rather than more afraid, which is strange, given what we have faced as a family and what we now know can happen at any moment. It's as if surviving the hardest thing – the greatest pain – frees me to live more courageously. You can crumble and give up. Or you can keep living and loving. I choose the latter.'

I'm so glad that I met Hannah. I wish I had met Matt too. There's something in his face that makes me think we could have been great friends, talking about books over a glass of wine. I feel something almost like envy for Matt and Hannah's life, until I mentally shake myself. What is the point of envying Matt and Hannah? Hannah doesn't even have that life anymore. I admire her so much for not allowing that loss to break her, for working so hard to get through it.

The positive changes that Hannah experienced in her outlook on life amidst her grief are an example of what is called posttraumatic growth. Traditionally, psychologists have studied the negative impacts of trauma and bereavement, the ways in which people are left broken and troubled, and the focus has been on how to return to so-called 'normal' functioning. In the past three decades, though, researchers have asked, What if people don't return to normal, what if they develop enhanced functioning instead? The term 'posttraumatic growth' was coined by two American academics, Lawrence Calhoun and Richard Tedeschi, who defined it as the aspects of positive, personal change a person may experience alongside intense suffering after a major life trauma.

The quest to find purpose in suffering is nothing new; suffering is as old as humanity, and efforts to explain it go back just as far. The Bible is full of examples of God using trials and tribulations to teach and test his servants. The most famous is the Old Testament story of Job, an upstanding and successful man who is felled by a series of disasters, including the loss of his wealth, his children and his health. Job struggles to understand why he is blighted and eventually learns that God will sustain him through both the triumphs and tragedies of life.

The world's greatest secular literature also frequently involves a life-changing event that transforms a person. In Tolstoy's *The Death of Ivan Ilyich*, Ivan is stricken by a crippling illness, and as he's dying, a kind servant helps him see that he's lived selfishly rather than with compassion and empathy. In Dickens' *A Christmas Carol*, the cold and mean-spirited Ebenezer Scrooge is visited by ghosts, and after a glimpse of his own future gravestone, miraculously becomes a warm and generous man.

Hollywood too has long deployed this theme, from *Born on the Fourth of July*, in which Tom Cruise's bitter, paralysed war veteran finds meaning in joining the anti-war movement, to *It's a Wonderful Life*, in which a suicidal Jimmy Stewart discovers that life really is worth living after glimpsing how things would have turned out in his home town of Bedford Falls had he never lived at all.

It was only comparatively recently that this concept leapt from the arts to the sciences and psychologists began to drill into what triggers personal transformation after a life-changing event. They looked at such questions as why some people alter their world views but others don't. How traumatic does the trigger event have to be? What are the ways in which people grow, and does this change last? Is the nature of the event linked to the type of growth? And what sort of counselling can help facilitate long-term positive outcomes beyond basic coping and adaptation?

It's important to note that posttraumatic growth does not occur instead of grief and pain, it's simply the accidental by-product of an experience that nobody would want in the first place. Hannah would relinquish every insight she's gained since Matt's death in exchange for his return.

There have been dozens of studies on the phenomenon of posttraumatic growth. In a survey in 2001, data was collected from almost two hundred survivors of sexual assault via a rape crisis centre. The women ranged in age from sixteen to fifty-two and about half of them had been assaulted by strangers. The participants were asked about positive as well as negative changes to their lives and those changes were assessed in four key areas – self, relationships, life philosophy and empathy. Just two weeks after their attack, most women reported some positive personal change, such as increased empathy, and over months, there was a realisation of their own strength and resilience. The women also reported negative effects, of course, such as the sense that they were less safe in the world, but over the two years of the study, the positive impacts became stronger and the negative feelings less powerful, although there was variability among the women depending on their personalities and the nature of their attack.

In another study, in 2004, 162 breast cancer survivors were monitored for a year and a half after their diagnosis. The mean age was forty-nine years and most had undergone a lumpectomy or a radical mastectomy. Most also reported positive psychological changes, and the number of improvements increased over the course of the study. Those who experienced the most personal growth were the ones who had actively thought about their diagnosis, ruminated on its meaning for their lives and discussed it with others. Some of the benefits the women reported were closer relationships with family and friends, appreciating their lives more, recognising their own positive qualities, becoming more spiritual, and realising that new possibilities were open to them.

More fascinating research emerged in the aftermath of the Westray Mine explosion in Canada in 1992. This killed twenty-six miners and was an enormous international news story at the time. Eight years after the disaster, researchers interviewed fifty-two family members of the dead miners, including parents, siblings, spouses and adult children. The findings grouped the participants into three clusters. Half of them were in the cluster labelled 'Rebuilt Selves'. They had found ways to make sense of their loss, they'd learned something about themselves, and taken comfort from the fact that the tragedy had changed public policy, so that a similar disaster was less likely to happen in future. The next largest group was tagged 'No Meaning, No Growth'. These were people who said they had not found meaning in their loss. They felt that their views about life had changed for the negative and that nothing good had come from the explosion.

The smallest group was called 'Minimal Threat, Minimal Growth' and it included people who agreed with the second group in thinking that nothing good had come from Westray, but nonetheless felt that their philosophy of life had not changed, either for better or worse. One participant summed up that group's view by saying, 'I'm not a person who thinks there is a reason for everything that happens, I think it was just meant to be.'

The Westray study is particularly interesting because it illustrates the range of ways in which people process tragedy over time, although easily the most common outcome was an experience of posttraumatic growth alongside the loss and bereavement.

There are too many studies to list in detail here but during the past three decades, experts have forensically catalogued how people have changed in the aftermath of events as varied as terrorist attacks, earthquakes, the loss of children, plane crashes, sexual assaults, paralysis caused by accidents, the birth of children with profound disabilities, cancer diagnoses, combat service, and even a shipwreck. The collected data from these studies shows that anywhere from 30 to 80 per cent of people experience posttraumatic growth.

That figure appears in numerous articles and books on the subject, and I must admit, it surprised me, because my opinion about how trauma affects people is mostly formed by daily immersion in the news. The media reporting on post-traumatic stress (a disorder characterised by flashbacks, depression and an inability to function) has become so prevalent that I assumed that any person who experienced a shocking life event would have a high chance of developing PTSD. The reality is that only about 10 per cent of people who suffer extreme trauma will develop PTSD.

Of course, that rate is higher in occupations that deal with tragedy day after day, such as police officers, paramedics and soldiers. Constant exposure to catastrophe has a cumulative effect and so the risk of PTSD is magnified. People in those jobs are trained to process what they see and are offered counselling to help mitigate the effects, not always successfully. But the good news is that if you're the victim of one terrible, isolated event, then once the initial trauma subsides, you have a drastically higher chance of experiencing posttraumatic growth than of developing PTSD.

These studies also demonstrate that the types of positive change people experience after adversity are many and diverse. They can be small ('I now notice the everyday beauty around me') or epic ('I changed careers and left my marriage'). Calhoun and

Tedeschi, having crunched all the available qualitative data, came up with five distinct categories of likely personal transformation: increased inner strength, an openness to new possibilities, closer relationships, an enhanced appreciation for life, and a stronger sense of spirituality.

Along with the types of change people are liable to see, researchers are also learning what makes people more likely or less likely to experience posttraumatic growth. By far the most important condition for growth is that the event itself has to be cataclysmic. It can't be a simple brush with death, like a car accident in which you break your arm. To spur growth, it must be seismic; it must shake you to your core and cause you to fundamentally rethink everything you believe. The higher the level of stress caused by the event, the greater the potential for change.

In the breast cancer study I described, the younger participants were more likely to experience higher levels of posttraumatic growth. The researchers concluded that this is because a breast cancer diagnosis is more unusual in younger women, and also more threatening and therefore more distressing. A younger woman may not have yet married or had children. She may be more concerned about her chance to do that after she's had breast surgery or chemotherapy. She may have small children and fear they'll be left without a mother. She may feel terror at the prospect of dying young and missing out on most of an average life span. This is not to say that older women don't also experience great stress, but that younger women suffer more, and therefore report greater growth.

There is also evidence that active contemplation correlates with growth, particularly writing or speaking about the trauma (as Hannah did with her 'overwrought' journals). In some cases, the emotions experienced are so strong that it's hard for the brain to process what occurred unless the victim actively wrestles to make meaning of it. Putting their feelings into words forces the person to clarify those feelings. And speaking with others who've been through something similar – social support – is another factor associated with high potential for growth, as Walter learned from the Dunblane fathers.

But while you may be able to control your social interactions and choose whether or not to talk about what happened to you, you can't control your gender, your past life experience or your personality, all of which also influence the likelihood of posttraumatic growth. Women experience growth more often than men do, probably because they're more likely to discuss their feelings with others. If you've had a life largely free from violence and sadness, that will also help: you'll be more likely to regard a sudden disaster as an aberration in the way the world works.

There are still many questions for researchers in this area: does positive growth dissipate over the long term as memory of the trauma fades? How influential in promoting growth is what happens in the first twenty-four hours after a disaster? The study of posttraumatic growth is important because if we understand the factors that cause and inhibit it, we can then change the way we behave towards victims – in the immediate aftermath on the part of police and the media; in the medium term for lawyers, court workers, psychologists and counsellors; and in the long term for schools, churches and families.

Hannah was fortunate that within a day of losing Matt, she met somebody who knew something about posttraumatic growth. This amazing guide set her on a path towards positive transformation and not collapse.

That guide was the woman Hannah met at the morgue when she identified Matt's body and whom she later saw for counselling. Her name is Wendy Liu. And within moments of meeting Wendy myself, I can see why Hannah found her so reassuring. She's around forty, petite, with short dark hair and a friendly face. Wendy speaks softly and resonantly, like a well-trained actor. There is indeed, as Hannah noted, something about her presence that makes you feel she's in control and that you can relax. She has an air of dignified competence. If I ever have to go to the morgue to identify the body of someone I love – and I very much hope to never test this theory – Wendy Liu is pretty much exactly who I would want to have with me.

We meet one morning in her office in the building above the morgue. Wendy's official title is Forensic Counsellor, New South Wales Department of Forensic Medicine. The department deals with up to four thousand deaths each year – everything from violent homicides to unexpected fatalities in hospital – and four other people perform a similar role to Wendy (including Jane Mowll, the woman who helped Juliet Darling). That means Wendy personally deals with hundreds of grieving families every year. She has seen corpses in every imaginable state: decomposed, beaten up, ravaged by cancer, savaged by animals, even pristine and bearing no signs of injury or illness. She has seen the lifeless faces of the young and the old, the rich and the poor, the beloved and the unmourned. It makes an impact.

'I'm aware of all the different kinds of ways I might die,' she tells me. 'I'm aware that my death and the death of those I love could be quick or not, horrific or not. But I also try really hard to be here, living in the moment.'

Wendy describes her current role as the 'interface' between the families and the forensics. Every day, she helps people prepare to face the reality of what happened to their loved ones. She may have to talk to them about the need for an autopsy or help them understand preliminary results. She often has to explain how the Coroner's Court works and why an inquest is necessary. She frequently accompanies stricken relatives to viewings.

Before this job, she was a palliative-care social worker. 'Was there something that attracted you to it? Or was it an accident?'

'It felt like an accident at the time, but it wasn't,' she says. 'I was a social work student. I turned up for an interview for my fourth-year field placement. At the end of that interview, my team manager offered me one of two choices: Would you like to work in medical rehabilitation or palliative care?'

Wendy didn't know what palliative care was, and the interviewer explained that it involved helping people at the end of their lives, when there's no curative treatment. Something about that clicked with Wendy.

'My dad died when I was young and the culture in my family was to shut it down. He died of cancer when I was seven, a very short illness, and then we didn't talk about him again,' Wendy tells me. 'What I've linked it to since is that I want to be part of a conversation with people, if they wish, around dying and death, and for that to be okay to talk about.'

From the first autopsy Wendy attended, it was not revulsion or fear that she felt: it was amazement and appreciation.

'Our bodies are phenomenal machines. I remember thinking: What a beautiful sight, the richness, the boldness of the colours, like a beautiful sunrise. I think part of life is appreciating the miracle of our bodies. I don't have a faith, but there is something intrinsically incredible about how we are put together and how we die,' she says.

Wendy has now spent more than fifteen years in death-related work, every day grappling with questions of fate, mortality and chance that most of us would find highly confronting. She stares life's most evil and senseless twists square in the face. But she also sees humanity's strength.

'Each day in this job I see love, sometimes anger and bitterness too. But mostly I see love in all its manifestations, including in loss – its most gut-wrenching form. I see the love that has bound families and lovers and friends together, and how it endures beyond the person's death, and how it feels alive and real in the room. Each day I witness the bareness of life, stripped back to who and what we love, and it makes our lives seem magical and heartbreaking and wondrous all at the same time,' she says.

Wendy copes with the traumatic and frightening aspects of her job because she has the sense that she is doing useful, purposeful work. She finds comfort in the knowledge that for the person who has died, no matter how confronting or cruel the manner of death, their suffering is over.

'I know that whatever death may be, it's an ending of some sort. So for me, I think there's a distance I can put between knowing that the death happened – and it may have been terrible – but it's ended for that person now,' she says.

The suffering, however, is not over for those who are left behind, and that's where Wendy feels she can make a genuine difference. Like Detective Graham Norris, she views her job as helping people to adapt to changed circumstances. That process begins before somebody even walks through the door of the morgue. Before that moment, Wendy will have already seen the corpse herself so she'll be able to describe to the next of kin, in great detail, what to expect. Being given this verbal description can neutralise what's going on in somebody's imagination, and help mitigate the shock of what they're about to see.

'Even seeing some horrific injuries, people have gone, "Oh, it's not as bad as I had imagined," and I think that's because our imaginations aren't bound by reality and so our minds can create endless, and often worse, possibilities,' Wendy says.

I am absolutely riveted by every word Wendy has to say. I know it's macabre, but nobody ever tells you these things. The first time most people have any idea of what it's like to go to the morgue to identify a body is when they have to do it. The mystery surrounding it surely makes the experience even more terrifying.

Wendy explains more to me, including the way that every deceased person is laid out identically, on a sheet with a green blanket covering them. If the person's own clothes are in a fit state to be worn, they will be dressed in those, but most people end up wearing a white hospital gown with short sleeves and a round neck.

'I start with a physical description of the room itself,' Wendy says. 'I'll point to the door and say that when I open the door, they'll see the room is divided in half by a low wooden barrier, and how the person is behind that barrier laid out with some bedding around them. I'll then talk about how the person looks. I'll describe individual features – the colour of their hair and skin, the way their eyes and mouth look, any tattoos or marks I see, any distinguishing features, really. I'll talk about how the person will be cold to the touch, because that can be a shock. All this positions people in the room so they can prepare for what they're about to see. It can help to stabilise people if you give verbal and visual cues about what is going to happen next and if you do it in a way that shows you care.

'As best we can, we clean their faces,' she continues. 'If there are some visible, even significant, injuries, it can be helpful for some people to see them. It means the injuries were significant enough for the person to have died. Otherwise some people think, But he doesn't look like he's been hurt, he looks like he's sleeping!'

If the injuries are particularly horrific, the morgue workers will cover them as much as possible. They always try to leave the hands out, if they can, as many people will want to clasp their loved one's hand when they say goodbye.

When someone arrives at the morgue, they are led to a private lounge adjoining the viewing room. Beyond the verbal briefing they're given before entering that room, Wendy doesn't have any particular plan.

'I think the essence of my job is to be kind and to know what I'm talking about,' she says. 'I meet people at their response. You have to go with what's happening in the room.'

According to Wendy, one of the most important ways to help people come to terms with a death, especially a cruel or unjust one, is to shift the focus onto the fullness of the deceased's life, not simply their final moments.

'Lots of people will come to counselling with trauma distress,' Wendy says. 'They'll want to know what happened to that person, what the details of their death were, who was there, who wasn't there, what the injuries were. So when you work with clients and they're fixated on how that person died, eventually you want to shift that into a fuller picture of their life. You want to hear about what that person was like for their life, not just the end of it. That's not the whole picture.'

'And do people want to tell you?'

'Yeah. I've been in viewings where people have pulled out phone after phone to show me photos and are like, "And this one, and this one," because in that room, it's the body of somebody they've loved but it's not that person in their entirety.'

This also means that, for some families, there can be laughter in a viewing, 'poignantly funny moments', as Wendy puts it, if the family is by nature playful. Wendy will carefully read the cues and if people look like they need encouragement to be themselves, she will try to help.

'I remember being in the viewing of a young child. The grandfather wanted to put a toy in the boy's hand but was a bit nervous about doing it. The grandmother was nervous too. They hadn't touched him yet.'

'I asked, "Do you want me to do it?" So I did the first one, put the toy in his hand, and then they wanted to add more. The grandfather took a deep breath, walked up, grasped the boy's hand, opened his palm and put his favourite toy in it. And it fell off. And we both looked at him and I whispered, "We asked you to do *one* thing."'

The family burst out laughing, and later the grandmother got in touch to thank Wendy for helping give them that experience.

'She remembered that moment of being in the room and being able to be with the child in a way that reminded her of what the boy had been like in the family, which was fun and light-hearted and silly.'

Humour also plays an important part in helping Wendy and her colleagues cope with their jobs. It's very common for people in death-related occupations to use black humour to relieve stress.

'We've each picked the trolley we want to come in on,' Wendy laughs, 'we have our trolley number, and that's one of our ways of coping.'

Not long after this, I can't stop coughing. 'Sorry,' I rasp, 'I've got that thing when you get a tickle in the throat and you feel like you're choking.'

'Well, you're in the right place,' Wendy immediately deadpans (yes, I did use the word 'deadpans' deliberately – sorry), and I laugh hard because it's so unexpected. I didn't anticipate laughing in this place. The context, a conversation about all the bizarre ways people can suddenly drop dead, makes it even funnier.

'But I haven't picked out my trolley yet!' I splutter.

I've never met anybody with as much firsthand observation as Wendy of ordinary days on which things went horribly wrong. It means my list of questions for her is endless. I want to know her theories on everything.

How often does the universe offer 'signs' that this is going to be a life-changing day?

Almost never, reports Wendy, including when the death is a suicide and you might assume that, in many cases, the family would have seen warning signs and been bracing for it.

'Every suicide in the city metropolitan area and surrounds comes to us. Almost every time you speak to one of the family, even if there was a history of mental illness or some ideation around suicide, when it happens it's a shock,' Wendy says.

'Is there anything predictable about the way people react to a traumatic death?'

'I can't hazard a guess about what someone's reaction will be. I've spoken to families where it has been a murder and also families where the death is natural and somewhat expected, and the grief response can be equally profound. It can be about the quality of the relationship, who is left behind, what was or wasn't said or done, all those factors.'

'How about the factors that make somebody more able or less able to cope with a traumatic death?'

'There can be protective factors, such as being an optimistic or resilient person, or being someone who has secure relationships in the family or in the bigger community. If someone has been in a relationship with the person who died where they gave deeply of themselves and where there was strong connection, it's not an easy path, but I think that can help. If you have an outside life that is more than the sum of just that person, that also helps. You can find meaning in something else.'

But Wendy also concedes that sometimes a person can have all that in their favour and still flounder for a very long time. The type of death, for example, can be enormously influential on the ability of those left behind to adapt. Suicides are notoriously difficult to process because the victim is also the perpetrator. The grief at the loss and the anger at its cause are tied in a terrible knot.

'Does it help if there is somebody or something to blame for the death?'

'I don't know about that, because if you look beneath the anger, more often than not there is sadness and fear. Anger may displace other feelings but the person has still died and the loss is still yours, that suffering and loneliness is still yours,' Wendy says.

'How about posttraumatic growth – is it real or is it a way of consoling ourselves that something good can come out of something bad?'

'Yeah, I've seen it. I've seen people who've gone through something so awful and somehow channelled it into living a fuller life where they are psychologically and spiritually transformed. Others get involved in changing laws or setting up foundations. Grief is many things but it can also be purposeful. In our sessions, Hannah was able to acknowledge the awfulness of what happened and together we tried to put it into some perspective. That took a lot of openness and courage on her part. She was really active in the process, really honest with herself and with me, which was great but also necessary. Ultimately, counselling is an act of hope. It's the hope that something might get better, and for that to happen, it requires something to change.'

Wendy's frontline experience backs the clinical research that for posttraumatic growth to occur, the event has to be seismic.

'It has to be monumental,' she says. 'Whatever happened to you, whatever that trauma distress was, has to be big enough to transform you.'

I ask Wendy for her theory about why we take so much care in our everyday lives to avoid illness, injury or death and yet we are all so drawn to tales of disaster or survival on the news.

'I think there's something about the "hero" that's certainly a narrative in our society, and we seem to need heroic figures to help us navigate dying and death. We create and are drawn to big stories where somebody has survived against the odds, where someone has gone through a death-defying feat and emerged. Or they haven't, but in the meantime, they've been heroic. I think it's because we fear the unknown and we don't know what it's like to die, so watching disasters on TV or reading about them in the paper lets us process death without dealing with the reality of it. And because we don't have enough conversations about the big stuff, about life and loss and fear, we end up approaching death with morbid fascination, like it's some dark awful secret or some big heroic event.'

Wendy also thinks that because most of the time, people can't easily talk about death and suffering, when a high-profile person dies unexpectedly, or a particular event is dramatic enough to land on the television news, such as Matt Richell's death, it presents an opportunity.

'I was in London at the time that Princess Diana died,' she says. 'I watched that unfurl and it was incredible to see. Not everybody is a monarchist but what you see is almost everybody being swept into this outpouring. We don't get to talk about the horror of death until something big like that happens. Sure, we are talking about somebody else's death or their violent death or whatever it may be. But we're also reacting to past losses we've experienced and our own feelings and fears around death. It's not just about the person who died.'

I cannot imagine doing Wendy's job for even one hour. I find it terrifying to think of having to be around dead bodies and to spend all day, every day with people who have experienced the worst thing I could ever imagine happening to me or a loved one. Wendy sees things so bad that they would be well beyond my deepest fears. I suspect she is putting limits on the detail of cases she's telling me about, knowing that as a 'civilian' I won't be able to cope. Wendy is truly remarkable, because somehow she's not only able to endure her job, she takes something positive from it. This petite, quietly spoken woman is so strong.

'I think if I can be in the moment with families, be really present, that seems to mitigate some of the impact for me, because I've done the best I can when I'm with them. I'm not left with lingering doubts about my part in it. And my job is amazing because it's constantly reinforcing the stuff that's important to me,' she says.

The stuff that is important to Wendy is living a life, both at work and at home, in which kindness and sharing are central.

'My connections with people are paramount. I think if I can serve myself and serve others well, if I can live in a way that I'm generally proud of, that is what is important,' she says. 'Through my work, I'm getting a pretty incredible free lesson about how to live well, if I pay attention.'

Recently, Wendy has had her views about how to live a meaningful life and her feelings about death seriously tested.

'Last year, I was diagnosed with breast cancer,' she tells me, 'and of course I took stock of my life, but I realised there's actually nothing I need to change. The important things are in order. I really feel like I live a wondrous life and what I have is enough.'

Don't be misled into thinking that by a wondrous life, Wendy means anything remotely like living in a swanky apartment with a harbour view, or dining at only the finest restaurants or possessing the looks of a supermodel. Wendy means that she once more has a healthy body after cancer treatment, as well as a healthy mind, loving relationships and meaningful work.

'For me, thankfully, my constant exposure to death has heightened the things I believe, and heightened my really clear ideas about what I want in a good life,' she says.

As in my conversation with Hannah, Wendy and I have spoken about gruesome and distressing topics and yet the atmosphere is utterly life-affirming. Wendy's wisdom and her grasp on what's important are extraordinary. Meeting her is memorable and thought-provoking, and as we near the end of our time together, she beautifully sums up the key lesson of her unique occupation.

'Somehow we need to be aware that we're mortal, that this time is finite,' she says. 'It's knowing this is all going to end, so let's make it matter.'

Seven

Ordinary Days

After my son's terrifying birth in 2014, life hadn't quite finished shaking me by the scruff of the neck. Six weeks later, he contracted viral meningitis and we were back in hospital. Two months after that, another blindside: not my baby, though, but instead his two-year-old brother. His day care centre noticed that his hands had a tremor. There followed years of visits to doctors, hospitals and therapists. My beautiful boy has various medical challenges to navigate, but that is his story and I will leave it for him to tell one day if he wishes. His little brother is now a rambunctious four-year-old who rules the house, defying his perilous arrival. He is developing 'neurotypically', which is how

I've learned the medical profession describes a child I would have previously called 'normal'.

And then, amidst all of that and when it seemed things couldn't get worse, my marriage of almost twenty years collapsed. It felt as if I must have done something wrong for the universe to turn against me so comprehensively. Like so many others, I too thought: I'm not a bad person, why is this happening to me? I was constantly braced for further grim news, fearing that I was about to lose my job or contract cancer, or that one of my parents would suddenly die. I felt as if I'd been hit by a bus and had staggered to my feet only to be hit by another bus. And then another.

When I started thinking about writing this book, I was frightened by what had happened to me, how thoroughly and rapidly my life had been upended. I was also scared of what appeared on my own TV program every night, how fickle and cruel the world often seemed. Mostly I was worried about what might happen to me next. What if something else went wrong? Something even worse? Walk through a children's hospital or read a newspaper and you'll realise there's always something worse.

Lately I've noticed among friends and even strangers a desire to stop watching or reading the news. The world seems so unstable and dangerous nearly two decades into the twenty-first century that it's easier to switch off and watch things that make us laugh or feel good instead of perpetually anxious. I completely understand that compulsion to look away, and so it seemed strange to me, as I embarked on this book, that I was choosing to do the opposite, to walk towards pain and suffering, particularly when there had been a modest measure of it in my own life. Now that I know more about how our brains work, I think perhaps it was an effort to impose control. If I could understand the things that rattled me, perhaps I could harness my own rampaging fear.

Even so, at the start of this process I wondered if I were making a mistake; if meeting the people in these pages and asking about the deep blows they'd sustained would finally tip me over the edge. I thought that perhaps all these tragic stories might crush me under their weight and I'd never get out of bed again.

Instead the opposite happened. They've given me hope. What people can get through is truly amazing. I have been stunned and inspired by the people in this book.

So often we refer to people like James Scott and Stuart Diver as 'survivors'. I'm not sure that's the best word. Survival implies an experience over which you triumphed, as if it's in the past. In the aftermath of something life-changing, it's not one event that you must survive, it's thousands of moments every day. It's going to the supermarket and seeing everything you don't need to buy anymore. It's having to comfort people, fear etched on their faces, when they don't know what to say to you because *being* you is the worst thing they could imagine. It's waking up every morning and knowing that you will never again hear the sound of your little girls' feet pattering down the hallway or feel their warm bodies squirming next to you in bed. To keep living life after such loss is not survival, it's endurance. We endure.

Many years ago, the American singer Patti Smith lost her husband suddenly. In 2016 she wrote in *The New Yorker* that her father had told her soon afterwards that time doesn't heal all wounds, but it does give the tools to endure them. 'I've found this to be true in the greatest and smallest of matters,' she wrote. I, too, am finding it to be true. I now know what some of those tools are. I believe in the power of 'being in the moment' and no longer dismiss it as a cliché worthy of an eye roll. I understand that the sight of the ocean meeting the horizon, or the sound of a champagne cork popping at the start of a dinner party, or the feeling of trying to stifle uncontrollable laughter at an inappropriate moment are some of the greatest joys life holds. They are the moments you remember and for which you yearn when times are not so good.

When I was in hospital after the birth of my second son, a friend sent me a beautiful shiny red box. Inside, wrapped carefully in paper and ribbons, were exquisite baby clothes and products. I asked somebody to close the box and put it on the windowsill where I could see it. My room was drab and sterile and there was little comforting about it. I was often alone, worrying whether my baby had brain damage and if I could cope as the mother of a disabled child. But every day, I looked at that red box and I thought, There is still beauty in this world. It meant everything. Sometimes, at the worst of moments, one small, beautiful thing to look at – a smooth stone, a flower, a beautifully crafted chocolate – gives the tiniest glimmer of hope.

I realised while writing this book that I'd been stuck on the question of how much truth lives in religion. I don't believe God exists and I'd therefore been subconsciously judgemental of those who do. Through meeting Louisa, Michael and James, I came to see that I'd been fixated on something pointless.

It doesn't really matter so much if religion is 'true' or not when it so clearly gives people hope, like the shiny red box gave me. Religion is an extraordinarily helpful tool at times of grief and loss because it offers both an explanation for the inexplicable and a supportive community. I find it incredible now to think that not one, but many religions have been able to devise frameworks with sufficient meaning to comfort billions of people. For me, it has been equally heartening to meet many people who've had the courage to face the worst that life can throw at them without faith.

While things didn't go swimmingly once I left the hospital, there was also joy and happiness amidst the worry and stress. This I found mostly in the kindness of others. If you had asked me before the events of 2014 which of my friends were my favourites, I would have said the funny, charismatic ones: the ones who take you to dinner and make you howl so hard with laughter that it fills your emotional tank. Even when you wake up the next day, fuzzy-headed from lack of sleep and too much wine, you feel great. While I still love company like that, I've realised that by far the most valuable friends are the kind ones. They may not be the most sparkling guests at the dinner table or the most memorable makers of wedding speeches. But my god, they are the ones you want to sit with you at the worst of times. They are the ones who know the right things to say and do, because their hearts are empathetic. I've come to believe that amongst all the good human qualities, there is none greater than kindness.

On my youngest son's second and third birthdays, my eldest son was in hospital. For the second birthday, my friend Ping told me not to worry about a thing and she showed up with a giant birthday cake designed as a construction site with little trucks and bulldozers driving on the icing tracks. Then for the third birthday, a group of friends came around at 8 am on a Sunday so the little one wouldn't miss out on a party. Melanie made a delicious chocolate cake with a number three on top in hundreds and thousands. Andrea organised lolly bags. It was just like a regular birthday party except for the hour. And when we wrapped it up around 9 am so that I could head back to hospital, Cathy took the birthday boy over to her house to play for the day.

George and Derek brought over curries for the freezer. Annabel took my little boy for a day so I could get some rest, even though she has three kids of her own to juggle. Ben dropped over a care package overflowing with homemade bread, pastries, trashy magazines and fruit. Mia and Caroline showed up with a week's worth of dinners, all labelled in ways to make me laugh. I assure you that 'Trump's "Grab 'em By the Pussy" Chicken and Vegies' was scrumptious. My colleagues at 7.30 sent a giant box of Lego to my house. Selina and Juliana made enough bolognaise to feed the entire cast of *The Sopranos*. Pam sewed hospital outfits for all the toy bunnies and bought them tiny suitcases to take to hospital. Sharon kept me sane by always being ready with practical help, any time, no questions asked. I asked friends to send some 'get well' videos that I could play to my son in hospital to help pass the time and cheer him up. Within an hour there were a dozen, and within a day, more than four dozen, even from friends to whom I'd not spoken much in recent times. Nadine somehow made her cat sing via Snapchat, something that was played over and over in hospital and caused a very miserable boy to laugh. When people show you kindness like that, it's hard to stew in self-pity, or any feeling that life is unfair.

The question of life being fair or unfair is one of the first things to drop away once you truly understand that you're as vulnerable as the next person to life's vagaries. The random distribution of misfortune is perhaps the only thing in life that *is* fair. No amount of money, fame, power or beauty can save you from tragedy, illness or death if they're coming for your family. I have a heaping plate of things in life that aren't fair – nice parents, a peaceful country, a good brain, sound health and caring friends. I didn't do anything to deserve any of that.

If you can see that much of what you have is due to chance, it becomes very easy to have empathy. It's like Michael Spence's son looking at all those people coming down the escalator in the opposite direction and wondering what the secret sorrow of their lives is. Understanding comes from experience, and so you may not necessarily understand what it's like to be Stuart Diver or Walter Mikac or any of the others. Empathy comes from imagination and so if you can envisage how readily your situation and theirs could be reversed, then suddenly it's easier to know what to do and how to act – that is, how you yourself would want to be treated in their position.

Of all the wisdom the people in this book shared with me, nothing has stayed with me more strongly than Steve Sinn's comments about accompanying. You may worry that accompanying people who are grief-stricken or suffering will be too hard, that it will be too upsetting to sit with somebody facing unimaginable pain or loss. And it will be hard, you can be assured of that. You may not want to do it. You may be terrified of saying the wrong thing, of making the situation worse. But in fact the only thing that will make it worse is your not being there. As Steve Sinn said, it's not about you, not about how inadequate or scared you feel. There have been times in my life when I've stepped back because I was afraid to step up. Now that I see that how I feel is irrelevant, I know I can be there.

During my writing, one of my close friends was diagnosed with terminal cancer. I heard Steve Sinn's voice saying, 'You have to accompany,' and I knew I had to, no matter how awful things became. I was scared; I worried about what I would see, about having to witness Mark in pain. But I had been there when we sat around at the pub laughing uproariously. I had been there in the passenger seat of his car when he dropped me home and we sat out the front talking with the engine running because we'd not yet run out of things to discuss. I had been there at dinners when he arrived with a lemon tart and a bottle of red. I had been there when he brought my children birthday gifts and I had been there when he texted me words of encouragement late at night when I was caring for my son in hospital. I had been there for those moments, and he had been there for me, so I had to be there when things weren't good for him.

It was not easy. I'd always text before I arrived, but sometimes I still appeared at awkward moments. Once, a nurse wanted to empty the bag that was draining fluid from Mark's lungs and she asked me to hand her various pieces of equipment while she did it. At these times, my natural inclination was to look away or to walk away. I really wanted to leave. But I didn't because Mark couldn't. If he had a cry, I had a cry. If he wanted to read poetry aloud, I'd listen (even though I'm not a poetry person). When I'd ask if he needed anything, sometimes he'd say a coffee or a cup of soup, but mostly he said, 'Just company.' I bumbled around at times, saying and doing the wrong things. I didn't go to the hospital often enough. I could have done more, no doubt, but the one thing of which I am certain is that I was there regularly, whether in person or on the phone. Just accompanying.

Every generation probably feels that it's living in a time of global uncertainty and existential threats. Things are perhaps no different now, yet something feels different to me. The world seems less safe than at any other time during my career in journalism, including right after 9/11. The news is more upsetting than ever – the indiscriminate, regular terrorist attacks that brutalise the hearts of cities; the fact that the Oval Office hosts an unpredictable bully; the way social media amplifies hate and shallowness. It feels that the ugliness of the world is front and centre all day, every day.

Watching or reading a lot of current affairs is probably always going to leave a sense of despair and fear. While I knew all too well beforehand that the news is highly selective in what it presents, I've become more aware through writing this book that what we see about shocking blindsides doesn't tell anything remotely like the whole story. Being struck by something awful is not the end of every good part of life.

Daniel Gilbert explained it well in his book *Stumbling on Happiness* by using the example of blindness: 'Blind people do most of the things that sighted people do and thus, they are just as happy as sighted people are. Whatever a blind person's life is, it is about much more than blindness. And yet when sighted people imagine being blind, they fail to imagine all the other things that such a life might be about.' Stuart Diver is not just the guy who was pulled from the rubble at Thredbo. Walter Mikac is not just the man who lost his entire family, and nor are Juliet Darling, Michael Spence, James Scott, Louisa Hope or Hannah Richell the sum total of the terrible things that happened to them. None of them is living a life they would have chosen but they're okay. They're better than okay. As Michael and Juliet pointed out, life isn't all one thing, it's not all happiness or all grief. These people are not frozen in time, they're not the people you might remember from the news. Life is much more complicated and beautiful than that.

What we see on the news is often the worst that life dishes up, but what happens next can sometimes be the best. We ran a story on 7.30 a couple of years ago about a woman who was the victim of a domestic violence assault with a hammer. Her teeth had been ruined and she said she didn't like smiling anymore because she felt ugly. After the program had gone to air, a dentist contacted us to say he would fix her teeth for free. It was hours and hours of work. Our reporter went back to see her when it was done and now her smile is beautiful and she flashes it all the time.

More recently, we aired a story about a shortage of rental housing in northern New South Wales after serious floods. It featured a struggling single mother who was about to have to move with her five children into a tent. A prominent Australian businessman rang after the program and organised to pay three-quarters of her rent for twelve months to help her get back on her feet.

Another night, we had a piece about disabled kids who were having a hard time meeting potential romantic partners, or finding fun, safe places to go without their parents. One of the mothers had paid for a disco out of her own pocket. The kids had an absolute ball, but there was only enough money for the one event. The Australian actor Ben Mendelsohn, who was in Los Angeles in the middle of a run of serious career success, happened to watch 7.30 online. He was so touched by the story that he contacted us and organised to pay every last cent for a second disco.

Acts of kindness are all around. They are often the reason why people endure the worst thing they could ever imagine. Not every individual life includes such a stark yin and yang of cruelty and kindness, hate and love, sorrow and joy. Some have more bad than good in them, and not everybody is helped by the generosity of others. Some people have to suffer through and rebuild on their own. But whatever the circumstances, an enormous number of bad stories do end better than you might have ever thought possible.

That's not to say there's always a happy ending in life. Some people do lose everything and never recover. Sometimes people hope they are at a new beginning when they are in fact right at the very end. Nothing about recovering from a devastating blindside is easy and often life is not better afterwards, it's simply different. And don't get me wrong – I'm still scared. I still worry about what might happen next. The difference now is that I'm fairly sure I will be able to carry on, as painful as it may be. The wisdom and experience of the people I've met has led me to believe that almost all of us are far more resilient than we could possibly imagine. My own life in recent years has given me hard evidence that I am way stronger than I ever thought. That makes me feel more optimistic about how I will manage in the future. The Under Toad will always be lurking beneath the surface of life, I'm just not so afraid of him. The next time his creepy hand grabs my ankle and drags me under, it will no doubt be as awful as it's been before. But I also believe that I will probably shake him off and keep going, with the help of others.

I wish that through studying all of this, I had some wise scroll to unfurl before you. Even the idea that I wish there was a 'lesson' shows how unwilling I still am, like most of us, to sail into the winds of fate head-on. I wish I could tell you how not to be the person who walks into the Lindt Café on the wrong morning, or how not to choose the fatal day to go for a surf. Of course nobody can do that, and if we thought about these things too often, we'd never leave our homes. To live life, we have to take risks, most of which we will never even know we're taking.

All I can tell you is that life is richer, kinder and safer than the news would have you believe. People are more decent. The things you think you wouldn't be able to survive, you probably can. You will be okay. There's really only one lesson to take from all of this and that is to be grateful for the ordinary days and to savour every last moment of them. They're not so ordinary, really. Hindsight makes them quite magical.

Notes

INTRODUCTION: STARING AT THE SUN

In late 2014, the news media was dominated I originally published some of these thoughts in a newspaper article: Sales, L., 'Ordinary Days That Go Disastrously Wrong Rattle Our Sense of Security', *The Australian*, 27 December 2014. http://www.theaustralian.com.au/opinion/ordinary-days-that-go-disastrously-wrong-rattle-our-sense-of-security/news-story/ea44aa7a1b19d49af5189989d47f3b71

In one fairly typical news month on 7.30 March 2016 archive for *7.30*. http://www.abc.net.au/7.30/archives/2016/730_201603.htm

'Uterine rupture in pregnancy https://reference.medscape.com/article/275854-overview

The novelist Iris Murdoch once wrote Murdoch, I., *The Sovereignty of Good*, Routledge & Kegan Paul, 1970, London.

ONE: THAT COULD HAVE BEEN ME

These strangers were forever united when a gunman Details of the
Lindt Café siege can be found in the report from the coronial inquest.
http://www.lindtinquest.justice.nsw.gov.au/Documents/findings-and-
recommendations.pdf

**In September 2002, Louisa Hope was diagnosed with multiple
sclerosis** Personal interview, L. Hope with the author, Sydney,
January 2017.

The chance of any Australian having the remarkable misfortune
The equation for calculating the probability of any one Australian being
both those things at once is: $(24 \text{ million} \div 18) \times (24 \text{ million} \div 23,000) =$
1 in 39 billion. This is based on eighteen Australians being hostages
in the Lindt Café, and the population of Australia at the time being
approximately 24 million, and approximately 23,000 Australians having
multiple sclerosis, according to the latest data: http://www.msra.org.au/
living-ms

Louisa's 72-year-old mother, Robin The account of what happened to
Louisa immediately before and during the siege is drawn from both
her interview with the author and five statements she provided to the
police, all of which were tendered as evidence at the inquest: transcript
of initial interview by NSW Police with Louisa Hope, 16 December
2014; audio statement with Louisa Hope, NSW Police, 23 December 2014;
additional statement by Louisa Hope to NSW Police, 17 January 2015;
additional statement 2 by Louisa Hope to NSW Police, 27 January 2015;
audio statement 2 with Louisa Hope, NSW Police, 12 May 2015.

For all recorded time, human beings have been fascinated Several
books and articles were invaluable in aiding my understanding of chance,
destiny and probability including:

Belkin, L., 'The Odds of That', *New York Times Magazine*, 11 August 2002, New York, retrieved from http://www.nytimes.com/2002/08/11/magazine/11COINCIDENCE.html?pagewanted=all

Bernstein, P., *Against the Gods: The Remarkable Story of Risk*, John Wiley & Sons, 1998, Brisbane.

Gilbert, D., *Stumbling on Happiness*, Harper Press, 2006, London.

Kaplan, E. & Kaplan, M., *Chances Are: Adventures in Probability*, Penguin, 2006, London.

Leigh, A., *The Luck of Politics*, Black Inc., 2015, Melbourne.

Rosenthal, J., *Struck by Lightning: The Curious World of Probabilities*, Joseph Henry Press, 2006, Washington.

Gambling can be dated back to 3500 BC Bernstein, op. cit.

And gamblers, along with people whose jobs involve precision Kaplan & Kaplan, op. cit.

Human brains have evolved to need predictability My explanation of the brain's preference for certainty and predictability, as well as its chemistry, draws on research discussed in Belkin, op. cit., and in the following books and articles:

https://www.psychologytoday.com/blog/your-brain-work/200910/hunger-certainty

http://www.patheos.com/blogs/tippling/2016/02/21/the-psychological-need-for-certainty-goddidit/

https://www.scientificamerican.com/article/are-we-addicted-to-inform/

In one study, monkeys were given the option . . . https://www.
scientificamerican.com/article/are-we-addicted-to-inform/

In another experiment, humans were found to prefer:

http://www.nature.com/articles/ncomms10996

https://www.forbes.com/sites/alicegwalton/2016/03/29/uncertainty-
about-the-future-is-more-stressful-than-knowing-that-the-future-is-
going-to-suck/#55c13894646a

The idea that everything happens for a reason Blastland, M., &
Spiegelhalter, D., *The Norm Chronicles: Stories and Numbers About Danger*,
Profile Books, 2013, London, p 75; Kaplan & Kaplan, op. cit., p 83.

The brain wants an explanation so it can satisfy Ronnie Janoff-Bulman
is one of the world's foremost thinkers on trauma and adaptation,
and much of her work explains these concepts brilliantly. I found this
article especially useful for this section of the book: Janoff-Bulman, R.,
'Assumptive Worlds and the Stress of Traumatic Events: Applications of
the Schema Construct', *Social Cognition*, 7(2), 1989, pp 113–136. http://doi.
org/10.1521/soco.1989.7.2.113

Take coincidence. You can find whole books devoted to King, B.,
& Plimmer, M., *Beyond Coincidence*, Allen & Unwin, 2003, Sydney.
(Page 26 of this work in particular refers to the common belief that
coincidence suggests there is more to life than random chance.)

After the Lindt siege, there were numerous anecdotes A couple of
examples can be found in these news articles (accessed 5 March 2017):

http://www.dailytelegraph.com.au/news/nsw/lindt-siege-i-should-
have-been-inside-the-lindt-cafe-that-day-reveals-maria-twomey/
news-story/877e42652e1ea13865dec6cb29322b1b

http://www.theaustralian.com.au/news/lindt-cafe-siege-how-martin-place-siege-horror-unfolded-before-me/news-story/631b0562dd57936
60b0932d878faa929

Such stories almost always appear after a disaster The *Smithsonian*
magazine included a clipping from *The Evening News* in an article about
famous people who should have been on the *Titanic* but weren't.
http://www.smithsonianmag.com/history/seven-famous-people-who-missed-the-titanic-101902418/?page=8 (accessed 21 May 2017)

The Law of Large Numbers explains why I relied on several books to
come to an understanding of the Law of Large Numbers, including:
Kaplan & Kaplan, op. cit.; Rosenthal, op. cit.; and Leigh, op. cit.

Say you dream that a friend died King & Plimmer, op. cit., p 43.

Yet Australia's population is 24 million The Australian Bureau of
Statistics has a population clock that is constantly updated. At the time
of writing, the Australian population was 24 million. http://www.abs.
gov.au/ausstats/abs%40.nsf/94713ad445ff1425ca25682000192af2/
1647509ef7e25faaca2568a900154b63?OpenDocument

If the chance of awful, random disasters The discussion about dread risk
and evolutionary biology are informed by: Gigerenzer, G., *Calculated
Risks*, Simon & Schuster, 2002, Sydney (particularly p 237); Ripley, A.,
The Unthinkable: Who Survives When Disaster Strikes – and Why, Random
House, 2008, London (particularly p 33); Slovic, P., & Weber, E.U.,
'Perception of Risk Posed by Extreme Events', *Risk Management
Strategies in an Uncertain World*, n.d., pp 1–21.

The news doesn't help you assess the gravest risks Ripley, op. cit.,
p 49.

In the months after the September 2001 terrorist attacks ibid., p 34.

. . . more than a thousand died in car accidents Bureau of Infrastructure and Regional Development https://bitre.gov.au/statistics/safety//

. . . minimax regret Blastland & Spiegelhalter, op. cit., p 56.

The top three causes of death in Australia Every year, the Australian Bureau of Statistics publishes the Leading Causes of Death data for Australia. The most recent figures at the time of writing are for 2015: http://www.abs.gov.au/AUSSTATS/abs@.nsf/allprimarymainfeatures/47E19CA15036B04BCA2577570014668B?opendocument

. . . around one in a thousand Australians died from heart disease In 2014, 20,173 people died of heart disease, out of an Australian population of 23,490,700, according to the Australian Bureau of Statistics: http://www.abs.gov.au/ausstats/abs@.nsf/Lookup/by%20Subject/3303.0~2014~Main%20Features~Leading%20Causes%20of%20Death~10001. To work out the odds, the population figure is divided by the figure for heart-disease deaths, giving one in 1164.

By contrast, the odds of any single Australian being one of the hostages The Australian population in 2014 was 23,490,700. Two hostages died in the Lindt Café siege. To calculate the odds, the population figure is divided by the number of hostage deaths, giving one in nearly 12 million.

. . . how much does the government spend on combating and treating cardiovascular disease The latest figures the government-funded Australian Institute of Health and Wellbeing could provide at the time of writing: http://www.aihw.gov.au/media-release-detail/?id=60129546452

How much does it spend on national security The latest available figures at the time of writing, from the 2015/16 Commonwealth Budget: http://www.budget.gov.au/2015-16/content/glossy/nat_sec/html/nat_sec-01.htm

We prefer to take a gamble that has Bernstein, op. cit.

Experts call those type of blindsides black swans My understanding of black swans and how organisations think about them was informed by:

Albin, G.F., 'When Black Swans Aren't: On Better Recognition, Assessment and Forecasting of Large Scale, Large Impact and Rare Event Change', *Risk Management and Insurance Review*, *16*(1), 2013, pp 1–23

Makridakis, S., & Taleb, N., 'Living in a World of Low Levels of Predictability,' *International Journal of Forecasting*, *25*(4), 2009, pp 840–844 http://doi.org/10.1016/j.ijforecast.2009.05.008

Masys, A.J., 'Black Swans to Grey Swans: Revealing the Uncertainty', *Disaster Prevention and Management*, *21*(3), 2012, pp 320–335 http://doi.org/10.1108/09653561211234507

He agrees to meet, and so on a slightly chilly Personal interview, M. Spence with the author, Sydney, November 2017.

TWO: WE'RE ALL IN THIS TOGETHER

I remember a very famous news photograph http://www.news.com.au/ national/northern-territory/walter-mikac-looks-back-at-the-port-arthur-massacre-and-its-legacy/news-story/89c9f4155c19e69f491de68ccf720f40

In 2008, newspapers ran a story about the death of Garry Lynch:

http://www.smh.com.au/news/national/garry-lynch-dies-at-90/2008/09/14/1221330652997.html

http://www.dailytelegraph.com.au/news/nsw/fond-farewell-for-garry-lynch/news-story/813f9ccd02140b80252769b5fb435584 (both articles accessed 28 March 2017)

'The one I think about Personal interview, W. Mikac with the author, Lennox Head, August 2016. For some of the account of what happened to Walter, I also used his own book as a reference: Mikac, W., & Simpson, L., *To Have and to Hold*, Pan Macmillan, Sydney, 1997.

'There was a lady I visited, Carol Loughton http://www.theage. com.au/news/national/a-daughter-gone-a-life-in-ruins/2006/03/31/ 1143441339508.html (accessed 29 January 2018)

'I read this article a month ago The article that Walter read is at http://www.smh.com.au/good-weekend/matt-golinskis-recovery-effort-20160527-gp5w9a.html (accessed 28 March 2017)

. . . he established the Alannah & Madeline Foundation You can find out more about the excellent work of the foundation here: https://www.amf.org.au/

The ripple effect of a national tragedy My thinking on these questions was partly informed by reading:

Nicholls, S., 'The Role of Communication in Supporting Resilient Communities', in Cork, S., (ed.) *Resilience and Transformation: Preparing Australia for an Uncertain Future*, CSIRO Publishing, 2010, Canberra, pp 181–187

Eyre, A., *Literature and Best Practice Review and Assessment: Identifying People's Needs in Major Emergencies and Best Practice in Humanitarian Response*, UK Department for Culture, Media and Sport, 2006, London.

One of the most common ways Western communities Whitton, S., 'Exploring the Role of Memorialising in Disaster Recovery', Winston Churchill Memorial Trust for Australia, Canberra, 3 Oct 2016. https://www.churchilltrust.com.au/fellows/detail/4086/Shona+Whitton (accessed 5 February 2017); Eyre, op. cit.

There are hundreds of thousands of online Barak, A., Boniel-Nissim, M., & Suler, J., 'Fostering Empowerment in Online Support Groups', *Computers in Human Behavior*, *24*(5), 2008, pp 1867–1883. http://doi.org/10.1016/j.chb.2008.02.004

. . . they offer some benefits that face-to-face interactions don't ibid.; Fox, S., & Fallows, D., *Internet Health Resources*, Pew Internet & American Life Project, 2003, Washington DC, retrieved from http://www.pewinternet.org

A 2017 Australian study asked people who donated The 'Australia Speaks' report was commissioned by Research Australia in 2017. The polling of donors was conducted by Roy Morgan Research.

A broader study, conducted the previous year *Giving Australia 2016: Philanthropy and Philanthropists*, Queensland University of Technology, & Swinburne University of Technology, April 2017.

Numerous studies, including after the 1990 Gulf War Holman, E.A., Garfin, D.R., & Silver, R.C., 'Media's Role in Broadcasting Acute Stress Following the Boston Marathon Bombings', *PNAS (Proceedings of the National Academy of Sciences)*, *111*(1), 2014, pp 93–98.

A study that started in 2001 looked at the mental health Updegraff, J.A., & Holman, E.A., 'Searching for and Finding Meaning in Collective Trauma: Results from a National Longitudinal Study of the 9/11 Attacks', *Journal of Personality and Social Psychology*, *95*(3), 2008, pp 709–722. http://doi.org/10.1037/0022-3514.95.3.709.

Research after the Boston Marathon bombing Holman, op. cit.

The good news is that communities are generally very resilient ibid.; Eyre, op. cit.

If good leaders put those things in place These articles informed my thinking of leadership in times of crisis:

https://hbr.org/2011/01/how-a-good-leader-reacts-to-a

http://www.oxfordhandbooks.com/view/10.1093/
oxfordhb/9780199653881.001.0001/oxfordhb-9780199653881-e-035

'You had to put what happened into some sort of national context Personal interview, J. Howard with the author, Sydney, July 2016.

John Howard dealt with more Australian loss of life In order to make this claim, I ran through non-wartime prime ministers myself and could not come up with somebody who had seen more death as the national leader. James Curran, professor of Australian history at the University of Sydney, verified this analysis in an email exchange. John Howard himself is a keen student of Australian political history – I also asked for his assessment and he thought my analysis was correct.

Howard often emphasised heroism Gillman, S., 'Heroes, Mates and Family: How Tragedy Teaches Us About Being Australian', *Cultural Studies Review*, *16*(1), 2010, pp 240–250.

His remarks after the 2002 Bali bombings National Memorial Service reflection, 24 Oct 2002, remarks of the prime minister. http://parlinfo. aph.gov.au/parlInfo/search/display/display.w3p;query=Id%3A%22media%2 Fpressrel%2FSBP76%22 (accessed 25 August 2016)

Canberra press gallery journalist Misha Schubert Schubert, M., 'PM's Arms Not All-embracing', *The Age*, 16 January 2005, p 17.

Howard's air of awkward authenticity The data about Howard's poll numbers and the commentary from former prime minister Paul Keating are reported in Hartcher, P., 'The Prime Minister We Had to Have',

Sydney Morning Herald, 28 May 2005, p 27. http://doi.org/10.1017/
CBO9781107415324.004

In 1968, Howard missed out on winning Leigh, op. cit.

. . . ultimately resulted in the deaths of forty-four https://www.awm.
gov.au/encyclopedia/war_casualties/ (accessed 2 September 2016)

As the marvellous Australian author Helen Garner Garner, H.,
Everywhere I Look, Text Publishing, 2016, Melbourne, p 212.

THREE: THE EYE OF THE STORM

His survival was so extraordinary that an American medical journal
Scott, J.G. & Zimmerman, M.D., 'Survival: Case History', *Annals of
Internal Medicine, 127*(5), 1997, pp 405–409.

'This week, I went and saw the movie *Sully* Personal interview, J. Scott
with the author, Brisbane, September 2016.

In 1991, James Scott was twenty-two years old The account of James's
experience is based on his own book as well as our interview: Scott, J. &
Robertson J., *Lost in the Himalayas*, Lothian, 1993, Melbourne.

Very quickly, the agent tied up a deal Carleton, R., Hardaker, D.
& Hogan, A., 'Survival', *60 Minutes*, Nine Network Australia, broadcast
9 March 1992.

***Frontline*, the brilliant satire** *Desert Angel* was episode 2, series 1 and
can be viewed here: https://vimeo.com/12697001

In February 2009, one of the most devastating bushfires Muller, D.
& Gawenda, M., *Black Saturday in the Media Spotlight*, University of
Melbourne, 2011, Melbourne.

One story I pitched was about children I have not been able to obtain
a copy of this story, so I am relying on my own memory. It would have
aired on Channel Nine, Brisbane, some time in 1994.

. . . I went on a raid of a cattle farm Sales, L., 'RSPCA Cattle', ABC
News Brisbane, 29 December 1994.

I was sent to New Orleans Sales, L., 'Tens of Thousands Unaccounted
for After Hurricane Devastation', *AM*, ABC Radio, 5 September 2005.
http://www.abc.net.au/am/content/2005/s1453048.htm (accessed
20 November 2016)

An American psychologist and academic Newman, E. & Nelson, S.,
'Reporting on Resilience and Recovery in the Face of Disaster and
Crime: Research and Training Implications' *Australian Journalism
Review*, 34(1), 2012, p 24.

. . . Amanda Gearing could not believe The description of Amanda's
experience on 10 January 2011 and in the aftermath: personal interviews,
A. Gearing with the author, May 2016 and July 2016, via Skype and
telephone. Amanda Gearing also kindly provided copies of the videos
she had taken of the rainfall so I could observe it myself.

. . . she was witnessing a superstorm For background information about
the cause and impact of the 2011 Queensland floods, I relied on the two
official inquiries into the events and their aftermath:

> Barnes, M., *Inquest into the deaths caused by the South-East Queensland
> floods of January 2011*, Office of the State Coroner, Queensland, 2012,
> Brisbane, retrieved from http://www.courts.qld.gov.au/__data/assets/
> pdf_file/0019/152362/cif-seq-floods-20120605.pdf

> Holmes, J.C.E. & Queensland Floods Commission of Inquiry,
> *Queensland Floods Commission of Inquiry Final Report*, 2012, retrieved

from http://www.floodcommission.qld.gov.au/publications/final-report/

... **thanks to a record wet season** Collerton, S., 'She's Back: What La Nina Means for Summer', 2011. http://www.abc.net.au/news/2011-09-21/la-nina-explainer/2902456 (accessed 8 July 2016)

... **from a population of about 500** http://www.censusdata.abs.gov.au/census_services/getproduct/census/2011/quickstat/GL_QLD1250?opendocument&navpos=220, (accessed 12 July 2016)

Even so, the scale of the loss and trauma Amanda's reporting can be read and heard at:

Gearing, A., *The Torrent: Toowoomba and the Lockyer Valley, 10 January 2011*, University of Queensland Press, 2012, St Lucia

Gearing, A., 'The Day That Changed Grantham', 2013, http://www.abc.net.au/radionational/programs/360/the-day-that-changed-grantham/4382482 (accessed 11 July 2016)

Amanda's study – from her admittedly small sample Gearing, A., Lessons From Media Reporting of Natural Disasters: A Case Study of the 2011 Flash Floods in Toowoomba and the Lockyer Valley, Queensland University of Technology, 2012, Brisbane.

The Black Saturday researchers asked survivors Gawenda & Muller, op. cit., p 204.

FOUR: THE THINGS THAT GET YOU THROUGH

In 1998, a mutual friend arranged for them The explanation of how Juliet met Nick, Nick's backstory, the circumstances surrounding Nick's

death, and his efforts to get medical help for his son Antony are based
on several sources, including an interview with Nick's partner, Juliet
Darling, as well as:

Darling, J., *A Double Spring: A Year of Tragedy, Grief and Love*, Allen
& Unwin, 2013, Sydney

MacMahon, P.A. (magistrate), *Nicholas Waterlow: Finding*, Glebe
NSW: Coroners Court Glebe, Glebe, 2014a. http://doi.org/10.1007/
s13398-014-0173-7.2

MacMahon, P.A. (magistrate), *Nicholas Waterlow and Chloe Heuston:
Reasons for Finding*, Glebe NSW: Coroners Court Glebe, 2014b.
http://www.coroners.justice.nsw.gov.au/Documents/waterlow%20
and%20heuston%20-%20reasons%20for%20findings.pdf

'Nick and I only had a very few arguments Personal interview,
J. Darling with the author, August 2016, Sydney.

Jane Mowll has a doctorate in psychology Mowll, J., Transition to a
New Reality: The Experience of Viewing or not Viewing the Body of
a Relative in the Context of Grief after a Sudden and Unexpected
Death, University of New South Wales, 2011, Sydney, retrieved from
http://www.unsworks.unsw.edu.au/primo_library/libweb/action/
dlDisplay.do?vid=UNSWORKS&docId=unsworks_9984

Juliet found the process of viewing Darling, J., 'On Viewing Crime
Photographs: The Sleep of Reason', *Australian Feminist Law Journal*,
40(1), 2014, p 113–116.

That speech made such an impact Dillon, H., & Hadley, M.,
The Australasian Coroners' Manual. Annandale, NSW, The Federation
Press, 2015.

'**Well, you tell your story** Personal interview, S. Sinn with the author, Sydney, September 2016.

'**It was the happiest I've ever been** Personal interview, G. Norris with the author, Sydney, November 2016.

The legal profession has made a big effort My understanding of therapeutic jurisprudence comes from:

> Wexler, D.B., 'Therapeutic Jurisprudence: An Overview', *Thomas M. Cooley Law Review*, *17*(1), 2000, pp 126–134, retrieved from http://heinonlinebackup.com/hol-cgi-bin/get_pdf.cgi?handle=hein.journals/tmclr17&section=12

> Wexler, D.B., 'Two Decades of Therapeutic Jurisprudence', *Touro Law Review*, *24* (May), 2008, pp 17–29.

> Wexler, D.B., From Theory To Practice and Back Again in Therapeutic Jurisprudence: Now Comes the Hard Part', *Monash University Law Review*, *37*(1), 2011, pp 33–42, retrieved from http://search.ebscohost.com/login.aspx?direct=true&db=a9h&AN=86195601&site=ehost-live&scope=site

Numerous studies in Australia and overseas have catalogued
The discussion about the ways legal processes can harm participants is informed by:

> Tait, G., Carpenter, B., Quedrelli, C., & Barnes, M., 'Decision-making in a Death Investigation: Emotions, Families and the Coroner' (author's version), *Journal of Law and Medicine*, *23*(3), 2016, pp 571–581

> Carpenter, B., Tait, G., Stobbs, N. & Barnes, M., 'When Coroners Care Too Much: Therapeutic Jurisprudence and Suicide Findings' (author's version), *Journal of Judicial Administration*, 24(3), 2015, pp 172–183

> Dillon & Hadley, op. cit.

A particularly confronting experience for many bereaved The UK inquiries are covered in Freckleton, I., 'Death Investigation and the Evolving Role of the Coroner', *Otago Law Review*, *11*(4), 2008, pp 565–584. The following newspaper articles report the investigation into practices at the Glebe morgue: Whelan, J. & Brown, M., 'Body of Evidence', *Sydney Morning Herald*, 24 March 2001; Patty, A., 'Giving Him the Horrors: Morgue Tests Shock Coroner', *The Daily Telegraph*, 20 March 2001.

. . . how do you apply therapeutic jurisprudence Some of these examples are drawn from Tait et al., op. cit.; Carpenter et al., op. cit.; and Freckleton, op. cit.

. . . a wonderful, sensible young woman named Jane Gladman Personal interview, J. Gladman with the author, Sydney, May 2016.

. . . coroners will generally resist declaring a death a suicide Carpenter, B., Tait, G., Stobbs, N. & Barnes, M., op. cit.

FIVE: A NEW NORMAL

'I know people think this Personal interview, S. Diver with the author, Thredbo, January 2017.

For women aged 45–54 The causes of death of Australian women in 2015 can be found in data cube 13 of the ABS annual Causes of Death report: http://www.abs.gov.au/AUSSTATS/abs@.nsf/DetailsPage/3303.02015?OpenDocument (accessed 18 February 2017)

. . . only 6239 men of Stuart's age This information was provided to me by the Australian Bureau of Statistics from the 2011 Basic Community Profile from Australia's census data.

But what about Stuart himself The data regarding the odds of a woman aged 47 dying in the next decade, and the most likely causes of her death, were provided to me by the Australian Bureau of Statistics, relying on their annual Causes of Death report.

There would be few Australians old enough My account of the Thredbo landslide and Stuart's experience draws on:

Diver, S., & Bouda, S., *Survival*, Pan Macmillan, 1999, Sydney.

Coroner's report into the Thredbo landslide: http://www.coroners. justice.nsw.gov.au/Documents/thredbo%20landslide%201997% 20-%20finding%20and%20recommendations.pdf (accessed 17 February 2017)

Thredbo Resort's website includes a history section featuring an account of the landslide: https://www.thredbo.com.au/village-life/about-thredbo/ history/the-road-collapse-of-97/ (accessed 17 February 2017)

A close-up image of his dazed face I was unable to ascertain who took this famous photograph. Stuart Diver thought it may have been taken by Paul Featherstone of the NSW Ambulance Service and then provided to the Australian Associated Press. It can be seen at: http://www.australiangeographic.com.au/blogs/on-this-day/2013/07/ on-this-day-thredbo-landslide

Of all the tragedies I've covered I first wrote about the inquest into the death of Private Jake Kovco shortly after it wound up: Sales, L., 'When a Mother Can't Let Go', *Sydney Morning Herald*, 5 April 2008. http://www.smh.com.au/news/national/when-a-mother-can't-let-go/2008/04/04/1207249460500.html (accessed 3 February 2018). I also relied in this section on notes that I kept from the military investigation and inquest.

. . . how well we adjust to a game-changer My understanding of adaptation and the factors influencing it was helped greatly by:

Lepore, S.J. & Revenson, T.A., 'Resilience and Posttraumatic Growth: Recovery, Resistance, and Reconfiguration', *Handbook of Posttraumatic Growth: Research & Practice*, 2006, retrieved from https://login.ezproxy.net.ucf.edu/login?auth=shibb&url=http://search.ebscohost.com/login.aspx?direct=true&db=psyh&AN=2006-05098-002&site=eds-live&scope=site

Wilson, T.D. & Gilbert, D.T., 'Explaining Away: A Model of Affective Adaptation', *Psychological Science*, *3*(5), 2008, pp 370–386. http://doi.org/10.1111/j.1745-6924.2008.00085.x

. . . a fixed level of emotional equilibrium and happiness called a set point The discussion of set-point theory draws from:

Lucas, R.E., 'Adaptation and the Set-Point Model of Subjective Well-Being', *Current Directions in Psychological Science*, *16*(2), 2007, pp 75–79. http://doi.org/10.1111/j.1467-8721.2007.00479.x

Hayward, H., *Posttraumatic Growth and Disability: On Happiness, Positivity, and Meaning*, Harvard University, 2013.

Headey, B. & Wearing, A., 'Personality, Life Events, and Subjective Well-Being: Toward a Dynamic Equilibrium Model', *Journal of Personality and Social Psychology*, *57*(4), 1989, pp 731–739. http://doi.org/10.1037/0022-3514.57.4.731

One person holds many different schemas The explanation of schemas is drawn from:

Park, C.L., 'Making Sense of the Meaning Literature: An Integrative Review of Meaning Making and its Effects on Adjustment to

Stressful life Events', *Psychological Bulletin*, *136*(2), 2010, pp 257–301.
http://doi.org/10.1037/a0018301

Janoff-Bulman, op. cit.

Janoff-Bulman, R., Calhoun, L.G. & Tedeschi, R.G, 'Schema-Change
Perspectives on Posttraumatic Growth', *Handbook of posttraumatic
growth: Research & Practice*, 2006, pp 81–99, retrieved from http://
rlib.pace.edu/login?url=http://search.ebscohost.com/login.
aspx?direct=true&db=psyh&AN=2006-05098-005&site=ehost-
live&scope=site

There are literally dozens of studies cataloguing Park, op. cit.;
Bulman, R.J. & Wortman, C.B., 'Attributions of Blame and Coping
in the "Real World": Severe Accident Victims React to Their Lot',
Journal of Personality and Social Psychology, *35*(5), 1977, pp 351–63.
http://doi.org/10.1037/0022-3514.35.5.351

When the brain keeps ruminating Janoff-Bulman, op. cit.

They pop up so regularly that *The Australasian Coroners' Manual*
Dillon & Hadley, op. cit.

'That's nice to hear,' says Mary Jerram Personal interview M. Jerram
with the author, April 2016, Sydney.

A coroner is basically a fact-finder The following publications informed
my explanation of the role, function and challenges of a coroner: Dillon
& Hadley, op. cit.; Tait, G., Carpenter, B., Quedrelli, C. & Barnes, M.,
'Decision-making in a Death Investigation: Emotions, Families and the
Coroner' (author's version), *Journal of Law and Medicine*, *23*(3), 2016,
pp 571–581; Freckleton, op. cit.

One of the cases that most affected Mary The accounts of the Cho inquest are drawn from:

'Coroner Urges Reform after Nut Allergy Death', ABC News 2012, retrieved 29 June 2016 from http://www.abc.net.au/news/2012-12-14/coroner-urges-reform-after-nut-allergy-death/4429000

Bodkin, P., 'Raymond Cho Decided "Walnut Cookie was OK", *Daily Telegraph*, 11 December 2012, retrieved from http://www.news.com.au/national/nsw-act/raymond-cho-decided-walnut-cookie-was-ok/story-fndo4bst-1226534415109

Gardiner, S., 'I Don't Think We're Ever Going to Know Why He Did That', *Sydney Morning Herald*, 14 December 2012, retrieved from http://www.smh.com.au/nsw/i-dont-think-were-ever-going-to-know-why-he-did-that-no-one-to-blame-in-tragedy-of-schoolboy-with-allergy-who-died-after-eating-walnut-biscuit-20121214-2bepl.html

SIX: OUT OF THE ASHES

In John Irving's novel Irving, J., *The World According to Garp*, E.P. Dutton, 1978, Boston.

No matter how miserable the weather The reconstruction of Matt and Hannah's life is drawn from various sources, including: personal interview, H. Richell with the author, June 2016, Sydney; Matt's Twitter feed, retrieved 20 July 2016 from https://twitter.com/mattrichell; and Hannah's blog https://hannahrichell.wordpress.com/ (accessed 25 August 2016)

On this particular day, Matt and Adam For this account I relied on the findings of the coronial inquest into Matt's death: Barnes, M.A.

(NSW SC), *Inquest into the Death of Matthew Thomas Richell*, Glebe NSW: State Coroners Court of New South Wales, March 2016, http://doi.org/10.1002/ejoc.201200111

Before long an ambulance was on the sand My description is based on Adam Simpson's account and a news photograph taken on the day: Hansen, N., 'Coroner to Find How Surfer Died', *Wentworth Courier*, 27 January 2016, Sydney, p 7.

Hannah distinctly remembers the overwhelming feeling Personal interview, H. Richell with the author, June 2016, Sydney.

Although a person dies in Australia every three minutes This was sourced from the Australian Bureau of Statistics: http://www.abs.gov.au/ausstats/abs%40.nsf/94713ad445ff1425ca2568 2000192af2/1647509ef7e25faaca2568a900154b63?OpenDocument

There is some research that shows it's ultimately psychologically useful Mowll, J., Transition to a New Reality: The Experience of Viewing or Not Viewing the Body of a Relative in the Context of Grief after a Sudden and Unexpected Death, University of New South Wales, 2011, retrieved from http://www.unsworks.unsw.edu.au/primo_library/libweb/ action/dlDisplay.do?vid=UNSWORKS&docId=unsworks_9984

The positive changes that Hannah experienced My explanation of posttraumatic growth, including its definition, the types of growth and the factors predisposing an individual to experiencing it, are drawn from:

Calhoun, L.G. & Tedeschi, R.G., 'The Foundations of Posttraumatic Growth: An Expanded Framework', in L.G. Calhoun & R.G. Tedeschi (eds), *Handbook of Posttraumatic Growth: Research & Practice*, Lawrence Erlbaum Associates, 2006, New York, pp 3–23, retrieved from http://search.ebscohost.com/login. aspx?direct=true&db=psyh&AN=2006-05098-001&site=ehost-live

Hayward, H., *Posttraumatic Growth and Disability: On Happiness, Positivity, and Meaning*, Harvard University, 2013.

Lepore, S.J. & Revenson, T.A., 'Resilience and Posttraumatic Growth: Recovery, Resistance, and Reconfiguration', *Handbook of Posttraumatic Growth: Research & Practice*, 2006, retrieved from https://login.ezproxy.net.ucf.edu/login?auth=shibb&url=http://search. ebscohost.com/login.aspx?direct=true&db=psyh&AN=2006-05098-002&site=eds-live&scope=site

Rendon, J., *Upside: The New Science of Posttraumatic Growth*, Touchstone, 2015, New York.

Tedeschi, R.G. & Calhoun, L.G., 'Posttraumatic Growth: A New Perspective on Psychotraumatology', *Psychiatric Times*, April 2004, pp 58–60.

There have been dozens of studies on the phenomenon Linley, P.A. & Joseph, S., 'Positive Change Following Trauma and Adversity: A Review', *Journal of Traumatic Stress*, *17*(2), 2004, pp 11–21. http://doi. org/10.1023/B

In a survey in 2001, data was collected from almost Frazier, P., Conlon, A. & Glaser, T., 'Positive and Negative Life Changes Following Sexual Assault', *Journal of Consulting and Clinical Psychology*, *69*(6), 2001, pp 1048–1055. http://doi.org/10.1037/AJ022-006X.69.6.1048

In another study, in 2004, 162 breast cancer survivors Manne, S., Ostroff, J., Winkel, G., Goldstein, L., Fox, K. & Grana, G, 'Posttraumatic Growth after Breast Cancer: Patient, Partner, and Couple Perspectives', *Psychosomatic Medicine*, *66*(17), 2004, pp 442–454. http://doi. org/10.1097/01.psy.0000127689.38525.7d

More fascinating research emerged in the aftermath Davis, C.G., Wohl, M.J. & Verberg, N., 'Profiles of Posttraumatic Growth Following an Unjust Loss', *Death Studies*, 31(8), 2007, pp 693–712. http://doi. org/10.1080/07481180701490578

That guide was the woman Hannah met Personal interview, W. Liu with the author, June 2016, Sydney.

SEVEN: ORDINARY DAYS

. . . the American singer Patti Smith lost her husband suddenly Smith, P., 'How Does it Feel', *The New Yorker*, 14 December 2016. https:// www.newyorker.com/culture/cultural-comment/patti-smith-on-singing-at-bob-dylans-nobel-prize-ceremony (accessed 3 February 2018)

Being struck by something awful Gilbert, D., 2006, op. cit.

. . . a woman who was the victim of a domestic violence assault Bowden, T., 'The Kindness of Strangers', *7.30*, 21 March 2016. http://www.abc.net. au/7.30/the-kindness-of-strangers-sees-domestic-violence/7264936 (accessed 3 February 2018)

. . . we aired a story about a shortage of rental housing McCutcheon, P., 'Murwillumbah Flood Victims Desperately Waiting for Housing Assistance', *7.30*, 3 May 2017. http://www.abc.net.au/news/2017-05-03/ homeless-murwillumbah-flood-victims-seeking-housing-help/8493510 (accessed 3 February 2018)

. . . we had a piece about disabled kids Robinson, L., 'Sometimes People Need a Little Help Finding Romance', *7.30*, 22 September 2015. http://www.abc.net.au/7.30/sometimes-people-need-a-little-help-finding/6796670 (accessed 3 February 2018)

Acknowledgements

I am indebted to the people who trusted me enough to talk to me for this project, some of whom have had more than their fill of journalists and all of whom have had more than their fill of suffering. Juliet Darling, Stuart Diver, Louisa Hope, Walter Mikac, Hannah Richell, James Scott and Michael Spence: I hope I have rewarded your trust by giving true and honest accounts of what you went through in a way that honours your own experiences and the lives of those who were loved and lost.

Thank you to the other people who were interviewed. I am particularly grateful to Her Honour Magistrate Mary Jerram AM, Jane Gladman, Wendy Liu, Father Steve Sinn, Noni Hazlehurst AM, the Honourable John Howard OM AC, Graham Norris, Dr Amanda Gearing and Lynn Houlahan.

For their additional assistance, I extend my gratitude to Angus Huntsdale at the NSW Department of Justice, Michael Wilson at the Australian Bureau of Statistics, Shona Whitton at the Australian Red Cross, Professor James Curran at the University of Sydney, Kirsty Thompson and Simon Bouda at the Nine Network Australia, Dr Denis Muller at the University of Melbourne, the Honourable Dr Andrew Leigh MP, His Honour Judge Roger Dive, Dr Jill Gordon, Johannes Leak and Adam Simpson.

Ben Ball was a dream editor: enthusiastic, encouraging and full of thoughtful suggestions that helped me enormously. Ben, I so appreciate your belief in me and your understanding of what I was hoping to do. Thank you also to copyeditor Meredith Rose for her excellent suggestions and tweaks. My gratitude to the rest of the team at Penguin Random House too.

This book could not have been written without my incredible researcher, Cathy Beale. Her attention to detail, ability to find relevant work, eye for an anecdote and unparalleled organisational skills saved me many hours. Thank you Cathy for agreeing to work for me on your only day off every week.

Deep thanks to my dear friend Pamela Williams for being my primary sounding board on the manuscript and for her remarkable friendship. There is no more generous and caring person that I know.

Other friends provided counsel and encouragement and I thank them with love: Julia Baird, Annabel Crabb, Callum Denness, Hugh Dillon, Mia Freedman, Benjamin Law, Lisa Millar, Caroline Overington, Sarina Rowell, Sally Sara and Cath Sullivan.

My friends, colleagues and family keep me going as always. Thank you to all of you but especially to Mum and Dad for so much support in recent years. You've been the greatest parents anyone could hope for and I appreciate every day how much you've done for me.

Finally, I wish kind fates on my sons, Daniel and James, and on days of both triumph and tragedy, I hope that they remember Robert Frost's wisdom about life: it goes on.